INTRODUCTION

Getting Started with This Book

Teachers have one universal wish that influences almost every instructional decision they make—to maximize their students' learning. Many factors influence teachers' ability to teach effectively. Contextual factors are often outside of teachers' direct control and include school climate and culture, district and state policy, geographic location, and community involvement, to name a few. What the student brings to the classroom in terms of prior knowledge, culture, experience, and skills also influences the end result. As teachers, we may have direct control only over what we bring to the classroom: our own knowledge, skills, experience, and beliefs about teaching. This book is about understanding these contextual and student factors that influence learning for students who are English language learners (ELLs). More important, it is about adding to teachers' repertoire to deliver the most effective instruction possible for the students they teach, with a particular focus on ELLs.

We have written this book to share with you—current or future teachers of ELLs—what we have learned from the many talented teachers we have encountered in schools serving children of diverse cultural and linguistic backgrounds. We also hope to share with you what we have learned from their students, who may have come to school fearful and hesitant about using English or another

1

language, but who proved capable of extraordinary achievements and of trusting that their teachers would teach them. In this book we offer a window into their teaching in the hope that you will learn from what they do and expand your own repertoire.

WHO ARE OUR PORTRAIT TEACHERS?

We have selected a few teachers to highlight—teachers whose stories capture those teacher factors that seem to make a difference between mediocre and excellent outcomes for ELLs. Our teachers were selected based on a variety of factors including the recommendations of school site principals, numerous classroom observations by research teams, and demonstrated positive student outcomes. Over the course of our research with a variety of schools, these teachers clearly rose to the top. Their reading instruction reached significantly beyond their district's standard reading curriculum. Classroom observations looked for those variables identified by our projects and previous research as effective practices. These variables include providing students with diverse opportunities for learning; offering direct systematic instruction in necessary readings skills; connecting with students' background knowledge, culture, language, and experiences; and creating a rigorous and collaborative learning environment, to name a few.

Each of these classrooms includes students who are in the process of acquiring English. The stories we share explore how these teachers helped their students learn to read according to challenging grade-level standards while also addressing their language learning needs. These teachers were able to help their students reach ambitious expectations. In some cases, the teachers were able to use the students' native language to support bilingual learning. In other cases, the teachers could not use this approach because of English-only policies in their state. Nonetheless, all teachers were very effective with their students.

We focus on reading and language arts instruction for several reasons. Language learning certainly occurs across all subject areas, but it is more focused and direct in reading and language arts. The ability to speak, read, and write affects students' success in all subject areas, making reading and language arts a critical area in which to apply instructional principles that will support ELLs. For more practical reasons, we selected this area of instruction because it is the area we have focused on in our own work with teachers—through professional development, teacher education, and research.

The teachers included in this book are real teachers with whom we have worked. Their involvement in our research projects led to descriptive data that we used to write their stories. Almost everything you will read was taken from data sources such as observations, interviews, teacher surveys, and student data. Since they participated in various different projects, we do not have the same data sources for every teacher. When necessary, we have filled in holes by creating or embellishing the descriptions of actual activities when our data did not provide enough description. In these instances, we drew on our memory and experiences in the classrooms to flesh out a more complete description of an activity, teaching strategy, or teacher-student dialogue.

WHO ARE ENGLISH LANGUAGE LEARNERS?

Before we begin, let us share some information about the students who are the focus of this book. Although almost all the ELLs in the classes we describe speak Spanish, ELLs across the United States are a diverse group, coming from many different backgrounds with widely varying previous experiences. Some are recent immigrants. Many students who are newcomers have little to no knowledge of the English language, and their families may have equally little experience with English. They may have had very little previous schooling and might have spent years in a refugee camp and experienced a great deal of trauma in their home countries before emigrating. On the other hand, they might have attended school in their home country and be quite well educated and ready to tackle grade-level material in the United States. They might have learned some English already. Whether or not students already know how to read in their first language makes a tremendous difference when considering how best to teach them how to read in English. We only need to learn how to read once. If we are literate in our first language, then we still need to learn sound-symbol correspondence in English, but our task is much easier. Even students who can already read in another language, however, still benefit from some explicit instruction to help them transfer the skills they have developed.

Many ELLs are born in the United States, and they also differ in various ways. They may be from homes where both English and Spanish or another language are spoken and are learning two languages at once ("simultaneous bilinguals"). Some are from homes where they and their families speak their native language almost exclusively, and they are learning English as a second or additional language ("sequential bilinguals"). We are just now learning more about "simultaneous bilinguals" and realizing that the process of learning two languages at once is different from learning first one language and then another. When students are in the process of learning two languages, typically they know fewer words in both English and their first language than their monolingual peers in either language. Yet, importantly, the *total* number of words they know could be the same or even higher. We should not worry when they code-switch—borrow from one language when speaking in another. It is not that they are confused or behind, or lack a language, or have a learning disability. Rather, we should realize that the process of becoming bilingual is different for them in some ways.

Also, the variations across social classes play a part in these situations. Whereas some ELLs are from wealthy or middle-class backgrounds, many others live in poverty, compounding the challenges they face. It is important to consider, however, that although their background experiences might not be the same as those of students from more affluent backgrounds, they still have had valuable experiences that can and should be used to support their learning. Even if they have not been to Disneyland, a museum, or the zoo, they have probably participated in family gatherings to celebrate special occasions and have family members with a range of skills and interests.

ELLs also differ in their previous schooling experiences, such as whether they have missed a lot of school or moved around a lot, attended preschool, or regularly attended one school with a consistent reading program. They may already have received some intensive support as part of a Response to Intervention (RTI) model, or been placed in special education. They may or may not have received some native language instruction.

Why do these differences matter? It is important not to make assumptions about children's backgrounds, so that we do not underestimate or overestimate what they can do and we can improve our ability to provide appropriate instruction. For example, students who already are literate in their first language can become bored very quickly if asked to learn to read with students who are not yet literate, even though they all may be at similar levels of English proficiency. These differences do matter.

Regardless of English language learners' home language, the methods of instruction addressed in this book can be implemented with all ELLs. We present solid, key strategies for teaching reading to students from "diverse" linguistic and cultural backgrounds.

Regardless of English language learners' home language, the methods of instruction addressed in this book can be implemented with ELLs. We present solid, key strategies for teaching reading for students from diverse linguistic and cultural backgrounds.

RESPONSE TO INTERVENTION

Response to Intervention is a model of early identification for students who experience academic difficulty in the general education classroom. This model also serves as a method of early identification for students with learning disabilities. Prior to the most recent reauthorization of special education law (the Individuals with Disabilities Education Improvement Act, or IDEA, 2004), students with disabilities often waited several years to receive assistance, causing them to fall further behind their same-age peers. Response to Intervention provides an alternative to this wait-and-fail model.

RTI's basic framework includes a multitiered approach involving a series of interventions whose intensity increases at each successive tier. Ongoing assessment is an essential component of this framework to determine whether instruction is meeting students' learning needs. The majority of research to date on Response to Intervention and early reading has focused on monolingual English-speaking students. Research focusing more on the learning needs of culturally and linguistically diverse learners is growing, but is still scarce. Given the increasing numbers of English language learners in U.S. schools, teachers must consider how an RTI framework may facilitate learning to read for these students. All but one of the schools we describe in this book (Bay Vista) were implementing RTI.

Tier 1: Effective Classroom Practice for All Students

General education encompasses the first tier of instruction. In this tier it is assumed that *all students* receive appropriate, rigorous instruction including a research-based reading program addressing the essential reading skills (such as phonological awareness, alphabetic knowledge, fluency, vocabulary, and comprehension). In most literature on RTI, this component is most often assumed. Such instruction increases students' opportunities for learning in the classroom. A majority of students do perfectly well with general instruction—approximately 80 percent of students at this tier. Schools conduct universal screening of students three to four times a year in the essential areas of reading to ensure that students meet necessary predetermined benchmarks.

For English language learners, teachers must consider several factors necessary for effective general instruction in reading. These include understanding how to make instruction and assessment linguistically and culturally appropriate for the students they teach. Teachers of English language learners must be aware of students' first and second languages and how to teach according to students' proficiency levels in both languages. They must consider students' cultural and familial experiences when planning instruction and assessment. Students' language and culture should be viewed as *assets* to instruction, rather than obstacles. In the classroom, effective teachers in Tier 1 recognize, tap into, and praise diversity. Students experiencing difficulty receive additional assistance in the classroom and are provided simple accommodations. When this assistance is not sufficient to bring students to proficiency, teachers consider additional Tier 2 intervention instruction.

Tier 2: Support for Struggling Readers

After receiving quality general reading instruction, 15 to 20 percent of students continue to experience difficulty acquiring specific skills known to be critical for later reading development, necessitating additional support on top of what they already receive in the classroom. These students will continue to receive general reading instruction and supplemental instruction with individualized or small-group support. In addition to universal screening three to four times per year, teachers assess these students' progress more regularly (perhaps weekly or bimonthly).

The literature often describes two methods of intervention instruction: the problem-solving approach and standard treatment protocol. Standard treatment protocol requires a standardized intervention for all students, most often provided by someone other than the classroom teacher and implemented outside the students' regular classroom. Conversely, the problem-solving model often works within a schools' existing student assistance or student study team, and the team develops a plan involving a series of classroom accommodations and modifications to the student's instructional program. The team objectively defines the problem, considers various factors that may have contributed to the problem, develops an action plan including evidence-based strategies for intervention, evaluates the plan, and monitors the student's progress. Both methods provide supplementary instruction to students experiencing difficulty with Tier 1 general classroom instruction alone. Intervention includes small-group instruction that is often provided by a general education teacher, reading specialist, or special education teacher.

Throughout Tier 2 instruction, progress monitoring provides evidence of the effectiveness of the intervention plan for individual students. Students who respond well to the intervention are not considered to have a learning disability. For students who receive intervention and do not respond—that is, their reading skills do not advance—the cause may be an inherent learning disability. This would be evidence that a referral for special education is warranted. Then the problem-solving team would initiate a referral, parental consent, and comprehensive evaluation.

For English language learners, the problem-solving model appears to be the more flexible of the two intervention approaches. Methods of intervention instruction should not only be tailored to meet students' basic reading skills but also address their linguistic and learning needs. Although RTI research involving English language learners is growing, more quantitative and qualitative research is needed investigating those contextual and student factors that most optimally support ELLs experiencing difficulty learning to read in a language they are only beginning to acquire. Schools should continue to monitor both the intervention and general classroom reading instruction for its appropriateness, fidelity of implementation, and sensitivity to students' language and culture.

Tier 3: Intensive, Individualized Support

Approximately 5 to 8 percent of students may require more intensive, individualized support. Districts vary in the number of tiers offered within their RTI model. In some instances Tier 3 may include a more rigorous intervention approach or referral for special education evaluation. In other cases, special education instruction would be Tier 4. The instruction level in Tier 3 may be provided in small groups or a more individualized approach than that used in Tier 2 and will likely occur in an alternative setting. Teachers at this level monitor students' progress more regularly than in Tier 2.

Ultimately, RTI is a viable alternative to the exclusive use of the traditional discrepancy model for disability identification. The discrepancy approach historically requires students to wait until a significant two- to three-year discrepancy appears between their cognitive performance and academic achievement. Use of this model and a lack of instruction embedded in culturally and linguistically appropriate methods leads to the over- and sometimes underrepresentation of English language learners to special education program services.

HOW TO USE THIS BOOK

Each chapter in this book focuses on one or two teachers and their students during reading instruction. We envision multiple ways that this book could be used to enhance the understanding of current or future teachers. Of course, you can read this book on your own—curled up at home with a cup of tea, in a coffee shop on the weekend, or at the beach in the summer—and reflect on how these teachers' stories relate to your own experience. Both novice and seasoned teachers will find something in each classroom to further their thinking about how to effectively teach ELLs.

Another option is to read it as part of a group of teachers. Many schools are adopting the practice of study groups for teachers, and this book would lend itself to such a format. Sometimes called professional learning communities (PLCs), teacher study groups, or lesson studies, these groups offer teachers the opportunity to come together after reading to share ideas about how the book's content might apply to their own school, classrooms, and students. Throughout each chapter and at the end, there are questions and activities that can be used in a PLC discussion group.

This book could also serve as a supplement to the textbook in a teacher education methods course. The classroom descriptions and activities included in the chapter will help university instructors bring theoretical and pedagogical concepts to life for prospective teachers. The questions and activities also fit well in small-group time during a course and provide a break from lecturing and whole-class discussion.

FEATURES OF THIS BOOK

Aside from the conclusions chapter at the end, each chapter in this book describes the school context, classroom, instruction, and students of one or two teachers who have been particularly successful in teaching ELLs. Two of our teachers were teaching in bilingual education models and were able to support both primary and secondary language development of their students. The other teachers taught in English and provided English-as-a-second-language support in the classroom while teaching the core subjects. Two of our teachers are special education teachers who provide instruction for students with disabilities who are also ELLs.

We have divided this book into three sections that reflect current thinking in a Response to Intervention (RTI) approach to prevention and intervention. The first three chapters describe core instruction in the general education classroom. In an RTI model, this would be Tier 1, the core reading and language arts curriculum. Chapter Four describes two teachers who provide Tier 2 supplemental intervention for students who are struggling with reading development. The last two chapters profile special education teachers who provide intensive instruction for students who have not responded to supplemental intervention. This could be considered Tier 3, or intensive instruction for students with significant learning needs. This book is not meant to be a step-by-step how-to guide for teaching ELLs or for RTI. In reality, there is no one model that will work in all schools.

Rather, we hope you will select elements of effectiveness from each teacher and think about how to incorporate them into your own classroom and school.

As you read each chapter, you will find stopping points along the way that encourage you to engage in reflective thought. Stop and Think boxes allow you to pause and consider the particulars of a classroom event or characteristic. We hope you will take the opportunity to examine your own practices and beliefs as you explore these teachers' instructional practices. At the end of each chapter, you will find activities and discussion questions that allow you to apply what you have learned to your own current or future teaching.

One

Core Instruction in the General Education Classroom (Tier 1)

CHAPTER

1

EFFECTIVE CLASSROOM PRACTICE IN A GENERAL EDUCATION SETTING

A SNAPSHOT OF THE CLASSROOM

Ms. Larson calls her students to the front carpet by table and passes out this week's class storybook. Maria and Diego await their turn to reach the carpet, both already clutching their copies of this week's story. "Okay, class," announces Ms. Larson. "Today is Monday, so I hope you're ready to go on a quick picture-walk through our story for this week. Take five minutes to walk through your book and see what it's going to be about. I think you're going to love this one. Remember to mark your favorite pages with a yellow sticky note so you can share them and your predictions with the rest of the class."

Maria and Diego both look eager to start sharing. They have marked their books already with several sticky notes. Ms. Larson gave them copies of the book last Friday so they could read it with a family member at home over the weekend. They have several stories to share with their friends about the connections they made with the story and the new words they learned. "Okay, class, who wants to tell us what they think the story is going to be about?" Much to Ms. Larson's surprise, both Maria and Diego, two of her quietest students, shoot their hands straight up in the air, hoping to be the first students to share. This is a big change, given that both of these students began learning English only last year, when they started first grade in September.

Ms. Larson is a second-grade teacher at Conrad Elementary School. New to Conrad this year, Ms. Larson brings a raw passion for working with children and a desire to continue her growth as a teacher. She is driven to seek new ideas, strategies, and ways of creating a safe learning environment, exciting classroom space, and challenging lessons. Her students see her as a supportive adult who believes in their ability, holds high expectations, and includes them as part of the teaching and learning process.

ABOUT CONRAD ELEMENTARY SCHOOL

The School Today. Conrad Elementary School is part of a very large urban school district on the West Coast, with an enrollment of approximately 850 students in kindergarten through fifth grade. The student population at Conrad is fairly representative of its surrounding neighborhood—primarily Latino (80 percent) and African American (20 percent) students. The majority of Latino families living in the area are immigrant families, with a large number from Mexico and the remainder from Central and South America. These families generally have a strong connection to their home countries. Most of Conrad's students are first- or second-generation Latino American and often the first English-speaking members of their family. Many parents work multiple jobs, live paycheck to paycheck, and often experience financial distress.

A Challenging Past. Not too long ago, the neighborhood around Conrad School experienced a high crime rate, where shootings, drive-bys, drug trafficking, and school lock-downs were fairly regular occurrences both on and close to the school's campus. This level of crime and violence led parents to keep their children home from school to ensure their supervision and safety. Chronic absenteeism and tardiness became the norm. Amid this constant unrest within the community, Conrad School, a local church, and other smaller agencies often served as safe havens for families wanting a safer environment for their children.

During this time the teaching staff at Conrad Elementary was primarily concerned with meeting students' basic needs, including food, shelter, clothing, and a safe home and school environment. Teachers felt unable to focus on academics when students reported being hungry and tired as a result of not having slept the night before or coming to school filthy or in ill-fitting clothes. Lack of resources and professional development in meeting the needs of a diverse student population—including providing intense English language development—hampered teachers' efforts to help their students achieve anything close to grade-level expectations. Few teachers implemented instructional intervention for struggling learners, and only a handful of students qualified for or attended after-school support programs. Families, many of whom spoke very little English, were unsure of their role in supporting their children's education. Many felt unwelcome at the school or unable to provide direct home support given their lack of understanding of teachers' expectations and their own family and work schedules.

A Time for Change. Conrad Elementary experienced a major turning point almost five years ago. Tired of its reputation of fostering poor student achievement, supporting minimum standards, and creating an unreceptive environment for parents, the school staff began focusing on high expectations, instructional support, and an inclusive atmosphere for families. Administrators, staff, parents, and students at Conrad have made great strides in beautifying the school and community by cleaning graffiti, painting murals, and planting trees. These efforts have made the campus a more welcoming and optimal environment for student learning. An outreach counselor and a social worker have joined Conrad's staff to assist with more challenging issues.

> *Tired of its reputation of fostering poor student achievement, supporting minimum standards, and creating an unreceptive environment for parents, the school staff began focusing on high expectations, instructional support, and an inclusive atmosphere for families.*

A team of school staff and parent volunteers address issues related to chronic absenteeism and students' physical and mental health issues. They meet with families on site, host weekly coffee gatherings, accompany parents and guardians to appointments in the community as necessary, and conduct home visits. The team initiated a Saturday Food Bank to help struggling families obtain necessary food items for their children. Through this ongoing local effort, the school provides parents with information on obtaining clothes, employment, and medical services within the community.

A recently formed parent-teacher association (PTA) creates opportunities for parents to actively participate in social networking and training events. Other similar organizations allow parents to voice their concerns about school decisions and provide input on the effectiveness and implementation of various support and instructional programs. The PTA developed a Conrad Family Resource Manual so that teachers could tap into family members' expertise and assistance for particular lessons, instructional units, field trips, and other authentic experiences. Thus far, parents at Conrad have assisted teachers in creating flower and vegetable gardens for the science curriculum, modeled cooking of favorite recipes to reinforce math concepts, shared personal stories and expertise for thematic units on immigration, family heritage, farm life, and Mexican and Native American culture.

In the last two years, Conrad School has developed and piloted a building assistance team (BAT) to improve general instructional practices for all students. The reading coach, principal, school psychologist, and special education teacher at Conrad are members of BAT. Team members observe teachers' general classroom instruction at least once per quarter to insure implementation of effective teaching practices. These visits are meant to be supportive rather than evaluative observations, to provide teachers with concrete, constructive recommendations for improving instruction for all students. After classroom visits, BAT members meet with teachers individually to discuss strengths and areas of need where further support might be required. The members of the building assistance team meet monthly to discuss general issues observed during classroom visits and teacher meetings. The team also reviews ongoing concerns reported during student study team (SST) meetings that month, where teachers discuss individual student concerns and develop action plans to address those concerns. Conrad is committed to improving instruction for all students by supporting teachers through additional professional development, coaching, and individualized support.

General Education Reading Instruction (Tier 1)

Although students continue to perform below grade-level expectations across academic areas, the school has made strides recently to improve the level of instruction, intervention, and support for the purpose of improving student achievement. Conrad has hired a full-time reading coach to support teachers' implementation of the district's reading program, benchmark assessments, and direct intervention services. The reading coach models intervention instruction for teachers in their classrooms, provides ongoing professional development, and assists in overall classroom intervention implementation.

The school principal recently allotted weekly time for grade-level meetings on Thursday afternoons, when students receive specialized instruction (in physical education or technology, for instance). During grade-level meetings, teachers discuss their students' needs and review benchmark data or progress monitoring data to improve general Tier 1 reading instruction. Minimum instructional days on Tuesday afternoons were added to allow teachers time for additional professional development in areas of need like English language development and enhancing reading comprehension.

Ms. Larson and Room 34

Meeting Ms. Larson. This chapter highlights the instruction of an extremely bright and enthusiastic second-grade general education teacher at Conrad Elementary, Ms. Larson. Originally from the Midwest, Ms. Larson lives in an apartment in the heart of the city fairly close to the school. Like many of her colleagues, Ms. Larson is a fairly new teacher to Conrad. Although it is her first year at Conrad, Ms. Larson worked as a primary grade teacher the previous year after completing her credentialing program. Coming to the West Coast meant learning new standards and curricula, but most of all learning how best to meet the needs of a more culturally and linguistically diverse student population.

Ms. Larson had some preparation through her university teaching program, but very little experience actually working with such diversity, including a large number of second-language learners. As she began preparing for the new school year, Ms. Larson asked herself and her new colleagues some tough questions:

How can I make sure my English language learners finish second grade with the skills they need to read and begin comprehending content in a language they are only beginning to acquire?

How can I provide literacy experiences for my students that will tap into their existing knowledge and resonate with their personal experiences?

How will I connect with students' families and encourage their participation in the classroom?

Continuing Her Professional Development. Although Ms. Larson had completed her teaching credential program, she was required to take additional coursework as an out-of-state teacher. She found it valuable to build on the basic foundation of her previous teaching credential preparation. Her parents, both of them elementary school teachers, continue to attend workshops and trainings to fine-tune their teaching. They find that even with thirty years of experience in the classroom between them, there is a great deal they can still learn to improve their teaching. As Ms. Larson's father repeatedly says, "learning to be a good teacher is a lifelong process." Ms. Larson is determined to follow in her parents' footsteps and learn how to become a better teacher for her students.

Ms. Larson's Classroom. Room 34 is located in a new building that was constructed during the summer. The first- and second-grade classrooms have brand-new desks, whiteboards, televisions, VCRs, and computer stations. The new building is a breath of fresh air for staff and a place of safety and learning for students.

During the previous summer, Ms. Larson attended a summer training held at the local university and sponsored by her school district to support primary grade teachers' reading instruction. The training covered the necessary components of early reading instruction for diverse learners and conducting ongoing assessments and instructional intervention with struggling beginning readers. The university professional development team provided numerous examples and active discussions on how teachers could set up their classroom for reading instruction and intervention support. For example, the team facilitated small working groups where teachers were encouraged to design an optimal classroom space that encouraged student collaboration, access to different forms of literacy, and promoted self-directed learning and exploration. It was obvious from the start that Ms. Larson wanted to put these ideas to work right away. Room 34 is a complete reproduction and extension of Ms. Larson's summer training!

The room includes amazing examples of center and class activities to support reading: students' work samples and print cover the walls. In one corner of the room sits a small writing table, fit with what looks like a tablecloth from home. The table includes a colorful lava lamp on one corner, a jar of freshly sharpened pencils, and a basket of paper. It serves as room 34's writing center. Large inviting pillows and bean bags in one corner of the room welcome students to read in pairs or on their own throughout the day. Another corner has a bookshelf stocked with library and classroom books, decodable texts, and audiotaped books for students to borrow and read. Ms. Larson makes sure to offer books of various levels of difficulty, so that students have the opportunity to read text at their independent and instructional level. She also takes time during classroom meetings held once a week to ask students for additional recommendations for books in the classroom's library.

Under the window on the opposite side of the room sits a long bookcase fit with numerous cubby shelves. There, Ms. Larson keeps a variety of activity tubs for students to pull out and take to their desks, sit on the carpet, or take with them to an activity table. Room 34 offers students a very flexible learning environment. Ms. Larson designs activities to reinforce her instruction during the week, provide practice for students in skills that need ongoing review throughout the year, and encourage students to extend their learning through more meaningful and authentic tasks.

Ms. Larson's Reading Instruction

Conrad Elementary requires its primary teachers to provide at least ninety minutes of reading instruction per day. Ms. Larson already is accustomed to

Ms. Larson designs activities to reinforce her instruction during the week, provide practice for students in skills that need ongoing review throughout the year, and encourage students to extend their learning through more meaningful and authentic tasks.

this time block and has added an additional forty-five minutes of intervention instruction in reading. Ms. Larson likes to take advantage of this time to work individually or with small groups of students working below or above grade-level standards. Her general instruction consists of the district's adopted reading program, thematic units, benchmark and progress monitoring assessments, guided reading, and instructional intervention.

In her previous teacher preparation program, Ms. Larson learned to design her teaching plans by keeping students' individual needs in mind and also making the content accessible to all learners. The mindful and meaningful (M&M) lesson plans she designed will be put to good use at Conrad Elementary, especially for her students who are predominately English language learners.

Mindful lesson plans take into account the following elements:

1. Students' English language proficiency levels in all four domains: listening, speaking, reading, and writing

2. State English language development standards

3. Students' primary language proficiency levels

4. Instructional objectives according to grade-level standards

5. Essential reading skills: phonological awareness, alphabetic principle, vocabulary, fluency, and comprehension

Meaningful lesson plans require Ms. Larson to

1. Scaffold instruction using visuals, realia, and the like
2. Activate students' prior knowledge
3. Increase students' motivation to learn (and decrease anxiety)
4. Provide instruction within students' range of learning (zone of proximal development)

Ms. Larson conducts benchmark reading assessments three times a year to determine whether or not her instruction is assisting students to meet grade-level expectations in skills such as reading fluency and comprehension. After her initial screening, Ms. Larson determines which students need additional support through in-class reading intervention and progress monitoring. The key to Ms. Larson's reading instruction is to provide students with multiple opportunities to learn throughout the day and in diverse and accessible ways.

Screening for Reading Problems and Monitoring Progress. During her summer training at the university, session leaders encouraged primary grade teachers to conduct weekly ongoing progress monitoring of their struggling readers. Weekly monitoring allows Ms. Larson to make necessary targeted changes to her instruction for the entire class and particularly for those students experiencing difficulty with reading. Ms. Larson saw an opportunity to use progress monitoring as a way to involve and motivate students by posting their "gains" on the classroom's bulletin board. The display shows a large mountaintop, and each student is represented by a billy goat attempting to "Climb the Fluency Mountain." Ms. Larson moves each billy goat according to students' gains each week,

> *Weekly monitoring allows Ms. Larson to make necessary targeted changes to her instruction for the entire class and particularly for those students experiencing difficulty with reading.*

specifically the number of words they are able to gain in reading fluency. To keep up with ongoing assessments, Ms. Larson trains her instructional assistant and a few classroom parents to administer individual reading fluency probes and update the classroom bulletin board. Ms. Larson makes certain to test the students who have been identified as needing additional support while her assistant and volunteers test the rest of the students in the class. Ms. Larson uses this information to gauge her own instruction. After assessing her students she often asks herself: What else can I do to help my students make progress? How might I change up tomorrow's lesson to make it more accessible? How can I provide my students with immediate support to meet their individual learning needs?

STOPANDTHINK

Monitoring students' progress is an essential component of Tier 1 instruction for all learners. Allowing students to monitor their progress can positively motivate them to improve their reading. What strategies might you implement to encourage students to monitor their own progress?

Providing Small-Group Reading Intervention. Students in room 34 begin their day in small-group instruction. Ms. Larson loses no time once students walk in the door and transition to their desks and centers to prepare for small reading groups. During this time students participate in individual or small-group instruction with the teacher, in addition to paired or small-group literacy-related activities. Ms. Larson uses this time to warm up her students early when they are fresh, to prepare them for later whole-group reading instruction.

Ms. Larson determines her instructional groups in advance based on students' benchmark and progress monitoring data and ongoing participation during whole- and small-group reading instruction, cooperative group, and independent activities. With her English language learners, Ms. Larson takes into account students' level of English language development and experience with literacy in both the primary and second languages. For all her students, she considers their parents' input about their children's individual needs.

During intervention instruction, Ms. Larson works with students on word and passage fluency tasks, including identifying word families, making and reading sentences with flashcards, repeated reading, and strategy instruction to facilitate reading comprehension. Ms. Larson wears a special hat with a stop sign pasted on the front during small-group instruction to signal the rest of the students that no one should interrupt her unless absolutely necessary. This instruction is strictly a time to focus on basic skills and supplements an existing reading and writing program embedded in authentic and meaningful activities.

Designing Peer-Assisted Learning Opportunities. When students are not working directly with Ms. Larson, they work actively at various centers around the room engaging in meaningful reading practices. Students spend approximately twenty minutes in each activity center before moving on to another activity. Often centers require students to work together in pairs or small groups on the same activity. Walking around the room, you see lots of activities that provide students with multiple opportunities for practice in essential reading and writing skills, including letter writing, computer use, listening to stories using books on audiotape, independent reading, and reviewing high-frequency words on the classroom's word wall. Ms. Larson changes or modifies centers as needed to match the thematic unit they are working on and to keep her students motivated. She wants to ensure that each activity appropriately reflects students' instructional levels, needs, and interests.

Developing Meaningful Center Activities. Initially Ms. Larson and her grade-level colleagues had a difficult time developing meaningful activities during small-group instruction, frequently opting for basic seat work including cutting and pasting tasks, puzzles, copying from the board, coloring, or tracing activities, just to keep the kids busy. The teachers decided to use their grade-level planning time to discuss students' needs and develop more rigorous and targeted activities that could support their students' reading, writing, and language development. Ms. Larson's center activities range in difficulty and authenticity. These activities definitely offer something for everyone.

One meaningful center in room 34 is a friendly letter writing center, where students write a letter to a soldier stationed overseas. When introducing this center, Ms. Larson shared her own sample of a friendly letter and reviewed the directions written on an easel at the table. At another center, Ms. Larson keeps word tiles in different colors for the various parts of speech (blue for nouns, red for verbs, and so forth) for students to make their own sentences. Students can write the sentences they make in a journal while color-coding the nouns, verbs, and adjectives. Another center requires students to read a book and complete a book review about the stories they read, so that other students can refer to the reviews. A specific word fluency center includes an activity called Up Against the Wall (see Exhibit 1.1). The goal of this activity is to help students quickly recognize high-frequency words, thereby increasing their overall passage fluency. Each center requires students to work actively in pairs or small groups in self-directed activities, allowing them to practice reading, writing, language, and comprehension skills.

EXHIBIT 1.1. UP AGAINST THE WALL

Goal: Students read and recognize high-frequency words with mastery and fluency

MATERIALS

- High-frequency words posted on the wall
- Sticky notes with students' names on them
- Timer
- Pointer

[Use the following dialogue to teach the activity initially.]

MODEL

Say the following:

"I'm going to set the timer for one minute. After I say "Begin," I will start reading the list of words as carefully and quickly as I can. After one minute, I will place a sticky note next to the last word I read."

NOW IT'S YOUR TURN

Say the following:

"After I say "Begin," you will start reading the list of words as carefully and quickly as you can. After one minute, you can place a sticky note next to the last word you read."

EXTRA SUPPORT

If a child has difficulty reading the words, read the list together and then ask the child to read the list alone.

Source: adapted from Haager, Dimino, & Windmueller, 2007.

Training Independent Learners and Student Leaders. During grade-level meetings, the second-grade teachers discuss the process of training students how to complete activities and develop written directions for each task. Like her colleagues, Ms. Larson takes the time to introduce and demonstrate new center activities and provides instructions at centers to help students if they have questions. In room 34, Ms. Larson takes this process slightly further by training her students to serve as activity leaders. Like Ms. Larson, center leaders wear special hats to signal who is in charge. She expects student leaders to watch over their peers, answer questions about activities, maintain organization, and help students remember to use their "inside voices" during small-group time. Training her students to become independent learners serves as a lifesaving strategy for Ms. Larson, who needs to spend intense and uninterrupted instructional time with her students at least four times a week. She reminds students of the guidelines for small-group instruction every morning.

Ms. Larson: If you have a question during group time, where should you look first?

Students: At the center.

Ms. Larson: Who else can help you?

Students: The activity leader.

At the end of small-group instruction, Ms. Larson faithfully checks in with activity leaders about their work, future recommendations, and their ability to keep the volume down. By the end of the term, every student in the class has had an opportunity to lead a center activity and thus share in the responsibility of contributing to the classroom community. Teaching and learning is most certainly a shared responsibility in room 34.

> *Teaching and learning is most certainly a shared responsibility in room 34.*

STOPANDTHINK

Learning centers are an ideal method for teachers to reinforce necessary skills and build in small-group instructional time with struggling or advanced students. How can teachers help train students to work with their peers and become independent learners?

Integrating Exceptional Teaching Practices. This year Ms. Larson received professional development training as a new teacher in Conrad's reading program. The reading program appropriately and strategically outlines how teachers should teach the key areas of beginning reading, including phonological awareness, alphabetic principle, vocabulary, fluency, and comprehension. However, what makes Ms. Larson's teaching exceptional is not necessarily her school's chosen reading program. What makes her an exceptional reading teacher is the manner in which she makes otherwise dry, scripted lessons her own by infusing essential strategies of effective teaching.

Ms. Larson recognizes the need to model, give examples, highlight overt relationships among concepts, emphasize the distinctive features of concepts, provide cues and prompts to use strategies and skills, offer ongoing feedback, and monitor students' understanding, all within a warm and supportive environment for student learning. When she notices her students' puzzled faces, Ms. Larson knows it is time to modify a task and give that extra instruction or practice for individual students when they experience difficulty. Instead of anchoring herself to her desk or to the front of the classroom, Ms. Larson floats about the room checking in on students and keeping them all actively on task.

> *What makes Ms. Larson's teaching exceptional is not necessarily her school's chosen reading program, but the manner in which she makes otherwise dry, scripted lessons her own by infusing essential strategies of effective teaching.*

Room 34 buzzes with an intense eagerness to participate and learn. Ms. Larson encourages students to speak often and contribute their ideas. Even when students struggle to find something to say or they make mistakes, Ms. Larson validates their ideas, incorporates them into examples, and helps steer students in the right direction. Ms. Larson's constant scaffolding and encouragement promotes high expectations and confidence in her students. She often tells her class that learning to become a better reader means you have to take risks and practice. Figures 1.1 and 1.2 show examples of several of these effective teaching strategies at work in a brief interactive journal activity between Ms. Larson and one of her students.

FIGURE 1.1 *Sample Student Letter*

April 20

deer ms. Larson

I want to tel you abowt my trip too mexico My famle went to see my abuelita who is bery old We had fun the end.

April 22

Dear Maria,

Thank you for telling me about your familyis trip to Mexico. Did you do anything special with your family while you were in Mexico?

Providing Extensive Vocabulary Instruction. Another example of Ms. Larson's teaching approach involves making connections with concepts previously reviewed, even when they are not covered in a particular lesson. She often finds the need to make connections when reinforcing vocabulary and language development, especially for her English language learners. Ms. Larson reviews

STOP AND THINK

Ms. Larson uses interactive journals to develop and model various skills. What exactly do you think Ms. Larson is trying to model in Figures 1.1 and 1.2? How do you think this method might assist English language learners?

FIGURE 1.2 *Sample Student Letter, Continued*

April 24

Dear Ms. Larson,

I helped my abuelita make arroz con leche. That's rice and milk. Its dessert. I love eeting it. What is your faborit dessert?

Love,
Maria

April 26

Dear Maria,

I love Arroz con Leche too. It's a very tasty desert and a favorite of mine too. How did you make it?

Sincerely,
Ms. Larson

vocabulary throughout all her lessons, even when certain words are not highlighted in her teacher's manual. In the following example, Ms. Larson does just this while explaining the meaning of the words *camouflage, prowling,* and *hunting.*

Ms. Larson: Some animals hide in plain sight, but they're hard to see because they have camouflage that helps them blend into their surroundings. Look at the animals in the picture. If you were outside, these animals would be hard to see because they blend into the background.

Student: Yeah, sometimes my cat, Cleo, sleeps on the couch in our living room. One time my mom sat on him because she said she couldn't see him since they're both orange.

Ms. Larson: Wow, yes, that's a great example! Cleo's orange fur made him hard to see on the couch even if he wasn't trying to hide. Many times animals try to blend in and hide on purpose by using their camouflage while prowling around for food.

Student: What does prowling mean?

Ms. Larson: Well, many animals can be found prowling around at night looking for food.

Student: They're hungry.

Ms. Larson: Well, if I'm a cat I might be prowling around the neighborhood because I'm hungry. *[Ms. Larson pretends to be a cat to demonstrate the example. Students begin shouting out their responses.]*

Students: You're sneaking around! You're trying not to get caught!

Ms. Larson: You're right! I might be prowling around looking for food trying hard not to get caught. I'm doing this because I'm hunting for my next meal. What does it mean to hunt?

Student: Animals need to eat. Some animals have to eat other animals for food.

Student: My cat loves to chase mice in the backyard.

Ms. Larson: So hunting is when animals look for and catch something, usually other animals, for food. Like cats trying to hunt for mice. Hunting is also used to describe when we want to find something we've lost or cannot see easily. Like when your mom loses her car keys and needs to "hunt" them down. She needs to search very hard to find her keys.

Ms. Larson allows her students to dialogue about the words they encounter in text and through discussions. She writes students' generated definitions on the board, uses pictures and manipulatives whenever possible, and builds on and incorporates students' ideas and examples in conversations. These conversations occur throughout the day, not just at the beginning of a special science or social studies unit or the first day of a new story they are reading. Talking about words and language is ongoing.

Promoting Instructional Conversations. Once students get settled, Ms. Larson immediately gestures to each table to sit on the carpet as a student passes out sets of literature books to every student. These books focus on a particular theme each week, which she reinforces in other activities and instruction during the day. Ms. Larson models appropriate reading and think-aloud skills, stopping often to clarify elements of the story and unfamiliar vocabulary words or phrases. She invites individuals, pairs, and whole groups of students to read portions of the text. Ms. Larson makes certain to seat her struggling readers next to more fluent reading buddies. All students have bookmarkers in hand to assist with tracking and sticky notes to mark their favorite pages for later discussions.

Although Ms. Larson often guides these discussions, she encourages students to lead these conversations and actively talk about the stories. She calls on each student with equal frequency to model reading, ask or answer questions, and share ideas. Ms. Larson encourages students to ask each other questions or comment on other students' ideas. Students often whisper their predictions and ideas with a peer to ensure participation. These instructional conversations help her students engage in text while

> *Carpet reading time is clearly a time for making sense of written text, learning vocabulary and concepts, and making connections with students' personal experiences and prior knowledge.*

improving their comprehension using a variety of narrative and expository writing. Carpet reading time is clearly a time for making sense of written text, learning vocabulary and concepts, and making connections with students' personal experiences and prior knowledge.

STOPANDTHINK

Choral reading is a popular method to use during reading instruction. How can you ensure that all your students, especially your struggling readers, actively read or participate during this time?

TEACHER'S VOICE

Creating an effective Tier 1 reading program for Ms. Larson's students required hard work, reflection, high expectations, collaboration, and planning. Let's see what Ms. Larson thinks of her first year at Conrad Elementary.

This first year was more about learning the school's reading program, getting to know my students and their families, setting up my centers, and conducting benchmark testing. The hardest part at the beginning was understanding how to interpret my ongoing assessments in light of my students' language and literacy background and integrate this information to improve my own instruction. Along with my day-to-day observations and feedback from parents, I feel the benchmark and ongoing assessments gave me a clear picture of my students' reading levels. As a teacher you can usually tell. But those conversations with parents and that initial testing gave me more perspective on how my students were performing and what aspect of my instruction was lacking. I feel now that my instruction is directed more toward students' individual needs.

The support I received from the building assistance team throughout the year was invaluable. Their observations and support helped me see things I never noticed about my overall instruction. They truly provided us with nonevaluative constructive feedback to help improve our teaching. Our reading coach helped us with planning and testing when we needed an extra hand and even came into our classrooms to model lessons. Our grade-level team found these visits so helpful that we started observing each other for lesson ideas and instructional feedback. This support has helped me concentrate on how I can respond to individual students more effectively, help students become independent and collaborative learners, and encourage oftentimes quiet and reluctant students to shine.

Setting up my centers provided me with more structure during small-group instruction, allowing students to work efficiently on their own. Although students were on board with how to work in centers at the beginning of the year, I found that they needed a review of how to work independently and collaboratively once we returned from winter break.

During this year I found working with other people an absolute must! I really believe that good teaching requires a collaborative effort. You can't do this job well on your own and realistically meet district and school requirements and address every student's individual needs. By working with my colleagues, we gave each other ideas for instruction and intervention and helped interpret grade-level and student-level assessments. Working with my students' parents enriched my instruction by making my lessons more culturally and socially relevant to their everyday lives. Students also got a big kick out of seeing their parents coteach with me for certain activities.

Our principal needed to be onboard 100 percent by creating the time for teachers to collaborate. Using our lunch and recess time to consult and plan was just not going to work. The principal worked hard at providing us with the necessary resources to work with students at varying levels of functioning. She was extremely hands-on, understood our programs, and cared about our students. With the assistance and input of the PTA, the principal spent time looking for creative ways to fund our requests for field trips, materials, assistive technology, and books.

Most of all, I found the biggest challenge this year was knowing how best to balance my focus on systematic instruction of necessary reading skills with an emphasis on reading for meaning that reflected students' everyday cultural, linguistic, and familial experiences.

Encouraging Native Language Support. At the beginning of the year, Ms. Larson had a difficult time getting her English language learners to participate during carpet reading. She knew the vocabulary and level of reading would be challenging, but she wanted her English language learners to participate in their oral discussions about the books they were reading. During Back-to-School Night, Ms. Larson spoke with their parents and together they decided that every Friday she should begin sending home a copy of the following week's read-aloud book. She connected with each parent to make certain there was an English-speaking adult, sibling, or cousin available to read and discuss the story over the weekend. She encouraged families to use their primary language when necessary to clarify the meaning of the text, compare English and primary language vocabulary and phrases, and help make personal connections with the stories. Once she began this practice, Ms. Larson saw an immediate change in her English learners' contributions during class discussions. Students were eager to participate during these conversations, giving them more opportunities to develop their English language and reading comprehension skills.

CONCLUSIONS

This chapter presented the general education reading practices of Ms. Larson, a young new second-grade teacher at Conrad Elementary. Ms. Larson's general education program provided students with a balance of whole- and small-group reading instruction and a range of experiences with text. Her teaching reflected practices known to be effective for early reading development and especially for those learning to read in a second language. In sum, these practices include the following components:

- Planning both mindful and meaningful lessons

- Designing activities that allow students to work collaboratively with peers

- Developing center activities that are meaningful and authentic

- Training students as leaders to facilitate learning experiences

- Encouraging families to provide in-class and home support whenever possible

- Encouraging appropriate English-language models outside of the classroom to support English language learning

- Promoting active meaningful dialogue using authentic text where students lead discussions that improve their reading comprehension as well as their overall English language skills

- Conducting universal screening and ongoing progress monitoring to inform instruction

- Providing explicit and direct instruction in necessary reading skills for students in small groups

- Using techniques that enhance learning, including making relationships among concepts, emphasizing the distinctive features of concepts, and providing cues and prompts to use strategies and skills

- Providing formal and informal instruction in English vocabulary and language use

ACTIVITIES

1. Individually or in a small group, develop three new activity centers that would help support your students' ability in any of the essential reading skill areas of phonological awareness, alphabetic principle, fluency, vocabulary, and reading comprehension.

2. The chapter outlines Ms. Larson's mindful and meaningful (M&M) lesson planning for her diverse learners. With a partner, design a lesson in any of the essential areas of reading reflecting Ms. Larson's M&M planning components.

3. Ms. Larson depends on the assistance of families to support the reading development of her students. She encourages them to use the primary language whenever possible during home literacy activities. Develop a brief presentation for parents, teachers, or administrators with examples and basic research describing why participating in home literacy activities is extremely important, regardless of the language in which they occur.

4. In the chapter Ms. Larson works with the families of her English language learners to support their English reading and vocabulary skills. However, not all families have someone at home who can provide appropriate English language models. Develop a pamphlet explaining ways non-English-speaking parents can support their students' general reading and English language skills outside the classroom. (Assume that this pamphlet will later be translated into other languages.)

DISCUSSION QUESTIONS

1. One of the biggest problems facing teachers is often the lack of time to do all the work they need to do in the classroom. Ms. Larson's school scheduled time for grade-level meetings and professional development days to help teachers with their planning and instruction. How can schools and teachers find the time for collaborative and individual instructional planning and professional development?

2. In her interview, Ms. Larson mentions struggling with applying her students' assessment results to changes in her instruction. This is a common challenge for many teachers beginning to incorporate benchmark testing into their routine and planning. Discuss how teachers or grade-level teams might work through this process more effectively.

3. Ms. Larson worked hard at the beginning of the year training her students to work together and become independent learners. What skills might teachers focus on to help train their students to work independently or in small groups? Describe how you would teach these skills to your students.

4. Describe specific methods teachers can use to support their English language learners during reading instruction and independent activities. How might these methods vary depending on students' level of English language proficiency?

5. How can teachers incorporate the assistance of families as part of the classroom's English reading instructional program?

CHAPTER

2

BILINGUAL KINDERGARTEN INSTRUCTION IN A DUAL IMMERSION PROGRAM

A SNAPSHOT OF THE PLAYGROUND AFTER SCHOOL

As the time for dismissal approached, more and more people gathered in the shade under the large banyan tree next to Bay Vista's kindergarten classrooms. Adults waiting included older men and older women, as well as others of all ages. The environment seemed a bit chaotic and unsupervised, but happy. Some children chased each other. Others played with little toy cars. A man was selling donuts at a table set up under the banyan tree. Adults chatted, bouncing babies on their knees. Clearly this was a time and place for them to congregate and share news. When the bell rang and children tumbled out of the classrooms,

Note: In this chapter, classroom observations were conducted by Janette Klingner and Josefa Rascón. This research was supported by the U.S. Department of Education, Office of Special Education Programs, grant #H324C980165–99C. The coprincipal investigators on the project were Beth Harry and Janette Klingner.

Ms. Chaney and Ms. Flores came outside too. The two teachers took the time to greet parents warmly and chat about how their sons and daughters were doing in their kindergarten classes. One parent showed Ms. Flores photographs. Someone else brought Ms. Chaney a donut, which she began to nibble right away. The teachers seemed to have an easy rapport with the parents and to know them well. They asked about health issues or when a baby was due. They shared stories about events from the day. And Ms. Chaney and Ms. Flores reminded parents to read with their children and ask which letters they had learned that day. It was not until the families had dispersed that they returned to their classrooms, chatting with each other about their shared students.

In this chapter we illustrate the instruction provided by two kindergarten teachers in a highly acclaimed dual immersion bilingual school. The examples are from field notes of observations conducted as part of a research study in which we were trying to understand the processes by which culturally and linguistically diverse students were referred to and placed in special education in twelve schools in a large urban school district (Harry & Klingner, 2006). We conducted several observations in selected classrooms, as was the case with the two classrooms highlighted in this chapter. Before we describe the teachers in these classrooms and depict their instruction, let us first provide a portrait of the school itself.

ABOUT BAY VISTA SCHOOL

Bay Vista is a beautiful school. (Bay Vista is a pseudonym, as are the names of all individuals profiled in this chapter.) As you climb the steps to the front of the school, you are immediately drawn to the large courtyard in the center. It is very inviting and nicely landscaped with large trees and tropical plants. The entire school was built in a Mediterranean style, with open, arched hallways around the courtyard. When you enter the main office, the impression is of bustling, purposeful activity. The small, cramped front office seems to be a hub full of parents, teachers, and students, all with seemingly urgent business. The office staff is friendly, efficient, and bilingual.

Bay Vista is a neighborhood school, rather than a magnet school, "created for neighborhood kids." Children not from the neighborhood must have a special waiver from the district to attend. The surrounding neighborhood and the school's demographics have gone through many changes over the years. As one staff member elaborated:

> When I started here in early 1983, the school was going through a change, because from what I gather prior to 1983 this school had much more of an elite school population. Then there was a change in boundaries and the population

became more mixed—still elite but also with lower social-economic families. Then there was a trend where more of the elite families were moving away and we were becoming more like a chapter one school. But I would say that within the last five years . . . a lot more families from higher social-economic statuses are coming, wanting their children here in our school. And I think that every year, it is a little more.

The principal confirmed this trend:

More affluent families have been moving back. I see an increasing number of young couples raising families that have been buying property in this area. We also believe that our program's reputation has increased tremendously with its high-caliber program. We have been able to prove that the bilingual education in this school has been a success. Our test scores have improved tremendously.

During the first year of the state's school grading system, Bay Vista attained one of the highest grades in the school district (a C) and received a cash award that was shared with every staff member. It was one of the only schools in the district to be awarded an A during the next year of the state's grading system. Their mean Stanford Achievement Test results for the year we began our study were forty-seventh percentile in reading comprehension, eighty-first percentile in mathematics computation, and seventy-second percentile in mathematics applications.

Demographics. During the first year we conducted observations there, Bay Vista had 1,379 students, of whom 27 percent were English language learners not yet considered fully proficient in English. The student population was 90 percent Hispanic, 8 percent white non-Hispanic, 2 percent Asian, Indian, or multiracial, and 1 percent African American. Almost 70 percent of the students received free or reduced lunch rates. There were sixty classroom teachers and eight special education teachers. Of these, 73 percent were Hispanic, 5 percent were white, and 22 percent were African American. There were two assistant principals and two counselors.

School Climate. Bay Vista has a positive energy that seems to pervade all the hallways and classrooms. Administrators and teachers are proud to work there and clearly feel fortunate to be part of a unique, acclaimed program. Teachers and administrators believe their school is exemplary. One assistant principal said:

I think curriculum-wise we've made a lot of innovative additions. And faculty-wise I think we are a very cohesive faculty. I think that when you look at teambuilding, this is an exemplary school. When you look at empowering teachers to take responsibility for their curriculum, I think this is an exemplary school.

A teacher shared:

We are a very good school. Our staff is very knowledgeable about everything that is going on. I can tell you as a parent I had a son who came here first through fifth grade who is now in a very academically oriented private school; he scored great on the entrance exam and you know by that it must be good. A lot of teachers have their kids or grandkids at this school. . . . That says a lot.

STOPANDTHINK

What factors contribute to the positive environment at Bay Vista? How is your school environment similar to and different from this one? What can teachers do to help create such an environment?

Bay Vista's Two-Way Bilingual Program. The administrators and faculty are very proud of their bilingual program. Every child in the school is in the same program: they spend 60 percent of their time in English and 40 percent in Spanish. Every child has an English teacher and a Spanish teacher. In the morning they start with one—say, the English teacher—and have language arts, reading, and the content areas in English. In the middle of the day, they switch over to Spanish and have language arts, reading, and the content areas in Spanish, and then math bilingually. Math is taught for forty-five minutes: fifteen minutes in Spanish and thirty minutes in English. If there are English language learners in the class, the English teacher uses ESOL (English for speakers of other languages) strategies and techniques.

> *Every child has an English teacher and a Spanish teacher. In the morning they start with language arts, reading, and the content areas in English. In the middle of the day they switch to language arts, reading, and the content areas in Spanish, and then math bilingually.*

The teacher continues:

We expedite the process of learning English as much as possible. The bulk of our ESOL students come in kindergarten, from homes where they don't speak in English. By second grade, the majority of our students are speaking English. Our English program is intensive and strongly emphasizes the fact that the kids need to learn English.

During Spanish instruction, students receive curriculum content in the home language. No one needs to be pulled out for these services. Most of the teachers are bilingual because, as the assistant principals explained, "We try to hire bilingual teachers as much as possible.

The goal of the school is for all students to be fully bilingual and biliterate when they move on to middle school.

It makes our program work better. It gives us a lot of flexibility because of the Spanish component." The goal of the school is for all students to be fully bilingual and biliterate when they move on to middle school. The school receives whole-hearted support from the local business community. The Chamber of Commerce openly supports bilingual education, noting that bilingual, biliterate employees are better for business (Fradd & Boswell, 1996).

In this chapter we highlight the experiences of two kindergarten teachers: Ms. Chaney and Ms. Flores. They taught the same students as part of Bay Vista's two-way bilingual program: Ms. Chaney taught the English half of the day, Ms. Flores taught the Spanish half, and they switched students at midday. They met frequently to coplan instruction so that students' lessons in Spanish complemented their lessons in English, and vice versa. During our observation period, they both had about twenty students in their classes. Both were excellent teachers, yet with different styles, and their students seemed to thrive.

MS. CHANEY

Ms. Chaney's family was from Jamaica, and some of her relatives were still living there. She had been teaching for three years. Ms. Chaney seemed to be an excellent, "with it," and efficient teacher. Rules and procedures were clear, lessons were well paced, engaging, and appropriate for the level of the students, and transitions were smooth. Ms. Chaney was clearly a caring, no-nonsense teacher, but without the exuberant warmth, humor, and bubbly enthusiasm of her partner, Ms. Flores. She kindly welcomed us into her classroom and always took time to answer our questions.

Our first visit to Ms. Chaney's class occurred when the school year had just recently begun. The classroom was colorful and well organized. One bulletin board was titled "A Totally Buggin' Class" and displayed a huge ladybug in the center whose spots were photographs of the students in the class. Another bulletin board was titled "We Know Our Names" and showed students' names formed of letters made by the students by gluing sand on them. All tables had two name tags at each place—a blue one for the morning students and a green one for the afternoon students. Many of these kindergarteners spoke Spanish in their homes and thus knew very little English.

Our visit began when it was almost time for students to switch classes; the English portion of their day was just about over. Students had just finished working in learning centers, and the teacher had asked them to clean up and return to their seats. She said cheerfully, "I see a table that looks beautiful!" When everyone was seated, she proceeded to hand out prizes to those students who had been awarded clips for good behavior. Students with one clip were given a sticker. With two clips, they could get a cookie from the cookie jar (vanilla wafers); with three, they could go to the candy jar; and with four, to the treasure chest. The teacher said, "Tim's team," and students came up. She had a comment for each student, such as "Three, candy; you did a good job today!"

Center Time. During another observation, this time in the winter, students again were in centers. On this occasion an intern from a nearby university was assisting Ms. Chaney. The class seemed to be humming with purposeful activity. The intern was sitting at a round table with five students seated around her. She was holding up letter cards, and the students then formed each letter with clay while saying its name and sound. The students seemed quite engaged in this task. It reminded us of the multisensory approach one of us had used as a special education teacher.

> *She was holding up letter cards, and the students then formed each letter with clay while saying its name and sound. The students seemed quite engaged in this task.*

Ms. Chaney was sitting at a kidney-shaped table with four students. She was reviewing letters and sounds with them. Each student had a paper that was folded in half vertically. They had written the letters "Cc" on one side and "Vv" on the other, and were drawing pictures underneath. While students worked, Ms. Chaney asked each one to say the names of the letters and their sounds. They were all able to do so.

At a little table off to the side of the room, a boy with earphones was listening to a book on tape. He seemed engrossed. Two boys were lying on a rug with a pillow, wrestling. A girl came over and sat with them—she had a glove with ice water inside and was holding this up to an obvious bump on her forehead. These three students then took out books and began reading quietly. Two other boys were at computers—the software they were using had colorful letters and pictures they were matching. Two different boys were coloring pictures with markers that indicated sequence (a seed growing into a plant). They proudly showed us their work and then went to show the intern. This kind of movement did not seem to be restricted. Then the boys played with the markers while waiting to switch centers. Three students were playing with puzzles and blocks (construction pieces that attached and looked like a ladder). They also had traditional building blocks available to them in this center.

At 9:46 AM a classroom bell rang, indicating that center time was over. Students quickly returned to their seats. We were struck by how well organized the room was. The intern reminded students to be quiet and turned out the lights. The paraprofessional (who had entered the room a few moments before) handed out lunch tags. Students lined up. Ms. Chaney said, "Louisa looks beautiful. I hear Albert talking. Let's see how nicely you can walk to lunch."

STOPANDTHINK

Learning centers are popular in kindergarten classrooms, but can be difficult to manage. What do you notice about the learning centers in this classroom? How might you use learning centers in your class?

Ongoing Assessment. We followed the class to lunch. While walking, Ms. Chaney asked Isabel, one of the students who had been at her center, what the letter *J* was. She told us that in her notes as well as in her head, she kept track of the letters every student knew and still needed to learn. She encouraged them to try to remember one new letter a day. She had drawn a picture on a dry erase board of "J, j" next to a jar of jam. She told Isabel that she was going to ask her the name of the letter after lunch. One of us whispered to Isabel that she had to remember *J* because that was the researcher's favorite letter (the researcher's name starts with *J*). So the entire way to the cafeteria Isabel kept saying *J* to herself.

> *While walking, Ms. Chaney asked Isabel, one of the students who had been at her center, what the letter J was. She told us that in her notes as well as in her head, she kept track of the letters every student knew and still needed to learn.*

She came up to us while we were walking back to the room after lunch and, with a big grin, announced, *J!* Back in the room, Ms. Chaney asked her the name of the letter, and she got it right (and seemed quite proud of herself).

> ## STOPANDTHINK
>
> Ongoing informal assessment that informs instruction is important. What do you notice about the example about Isabel? In what ways do you informally assess your students? How do you keep track of assessment results? How do you use this information when teaching?

Thematic Instruction. A few weeks later, in early March, we observed again. The students were sitting in the meeting area listening to Ms. Chaney read the book *Chicka, Chicka, Boom, Boom* (Martin, Archambault, & Ehlert, 1989). The story is about letters climbing to the top of a coconut tree (such as, "A told B, and B told C: I'll meet you at the top of the coconut tree"). The students seemed to be attending closely and enjoying it. When Ms. Chaney got to parts of the story they knew, they joined her, "reading" the story aloud with her. As they read different letters, Ms. Chaney called students' names that began with that letter. For instance, when the letter *E* was climbing the tree, she said, "Estela's letter is climbing up the coconut tree!" The students seemed to be especially delighted by this.

Once she had finished reading the book, she quickly drew a coconut palm tree on the board. She then drew coconuts climbing up the tree, and on each coconut she wrote a letter of her name. She explained to the students that they needed to do the same. The students went back to their seats, and Ms. Chaney passed out the papers for them to use. Some children did not understand what to do, so the teacher went to the board where she had drawn the coconut tree and asked for everyone's attention. She then modeled for them again how to write their names with one letter in each coconut. She asked if everyone understood before she began roaming around the room offering assistance to individual students. She then collected all the papers, and the students lined up for lunch.

When the class got back from lunch they began a new but related activity, labeling the parts of the tree. Ms. Chaney showed the students a big drawing of a tree. She asked them what parts they thought a tree would have. The students were all sitting in the meeting area attentively raising their hands, seemingly anxious to respond. Ms. Chaney called on a student who said, "Leafs." Ms. Chaney said, "Yes, leaves," and then labeled that part of the tree. Another student offered, "Trunk" and she added the label. Michael said, "Parrot." Ms. Chaney smiled and gently corrected him, "A parrot? A parrot *lives* in a tree, but it is not part of a tree." Then she asked him for another idea, while pointing to the tree's roots.

STOPANDTHINK

Research has shown that thematic instruction is beneficial for English language learners. Why do you think this is so? Even if you do not teach using formal thematic units, in what ways can you apply the principles of thematic instruction to your teaching?

Michael responded, "Roots!" After they had labeled the parts of the tree, she asked them what the tree needed in order to live. The students mentioned water and sunlight. She enthused, "Yes, that's exactly right!" and informed them that next they would be checking on their bean plants to see if they needed water. The whole class lined up and went out to check on their plants.

When they came back inside they gathered in the meeting area once again, and the teacher now read aloud *Jack and the Beanstalk*. Again the students listened attentively and seemed engaged in the story. Ms. Chaney asked them to predict what would happen and asked questions to check their understanding. She asked them whether this was a true story or a make-believe story. The students replied in unison, "Make-believe!" She added, "Yes, it was a make-believe story, and it was a fairy tale."

MS. FLORES

Ms. Flores is Latina and in her early thirties. She is an outstanding teacher, one of the best we have ever observed. She was very animated and expressive. Her lessons were marked by humor, enthusiasm, and imagination. She laughed a lot. She always seemed to be having fun, and this helped make learning fun for everyone. She clearly had an excellent rapport with her students and established close personal relationships with them, as if they were family. You could not help but feel warm and fuzzy just by sitting in her classroom.

She was very animated and expressive. Her lessons were marked by humor, enthusiasm, and imagination. She laughed a lot. She always seemed to be having fun, and this helped make learning fun for everyone. She clearly had an excellent rapport with her students and established close personal relationships with them, as if they were family.

We first observed Ms. Flores's classroom soon after the school year had begun in September. When we entered the room, the lights were out. The teacher turned the lights back on and said, *Yo voy a contar de uno a tres. Que no voy a ponerme triste mañana.* [I am going to count from one to three, so that I won't become sad tomorrow.] She said that she wanted to see *niños contentos* [happy children] when she opened her eyes—she counted to three with her eyes closed, covered, and then opened them to see the kids all smiling, looking up at her.

Learning the Letter E. Ms. Flores wrote three words on the board: *espinaca, ensalada,* and *elotes* [spinach, salad, and corn]. A chart already posted on the board had an incomplete sentence written on it: *El elefante come_____.* [The elephant eats _____.] She asked, *¿Quién ve la letra* E? [Who sees the letter *E?]* Ms. Flores called a student up to the board and handed him a yardstick. He pointed to *E* in the words on the board with the yardstick as the teacher circled them. Then she asked about the letter *A* (though the focus of the day's lesson was *E,* the teacher asked about *A* to review what the students had learned previously). A student exclaimed, *¡Yo vi una!* [I see one!] Almost all students were raising their hands exuberantly. The teacher reminded them to raise their hands quietly and then called a student to come up and point out the letter *A*—again she circled them, but this time in another color.

We noticed that the students all had cute elephants that they had made themselves on their desks. The teacher next asked (in Spanish) what elephants eat. Freddie said, "Broccoli" (in English). She responded, *Sí,* but that she wanted words that start with *E,* like *escoba* [broom]. She quickly drew a picture of a broom to provide a visual cue for Freddie (Freddie speaks English at home and is just beginning to learn Spanish as a second language). Michael volunteered, *El elefante come escoba.* Another student responded that an elefante can't eat an *escoba.* The teacher said, *No importa.* [That's not important.] Another student suggested, *Cama.* [Bed.] The teacher said, *No, escucha: elefante, cama,* emphasizing the first *E* in *elefante.* Another student said, *Escuela.* The teacher drew a picture and laughed. (She seemed to be having fun, and was so expressive.) Freddie asked, *¿Niño?* [Boy?] The teacher said, *Mira.* [Look.] She wrote *niño* on the board and asked, *¿Empieza con* E? [Does it begin with *E?]* Freddie responded, "No." Ms. Flores went and got a star out of an envelope and handed it to Freddie. She whispered to him *estrella* [star], again emphasizing the beginning sound. She asked, *¿Empieza con* E? He answered, *"¡Sí!"* and she wrote *estrella* on the board. Freddie had a big smile on his face, seemingly feeling proud of his contribution. This scaffolding was very well done.

STOPANDTHINK

In what ways does Ms. Flores scaffold students' understanding in this lesson? Freddie is unlike most of his classmates in that he speaks very little Spanish. How does the teacher support him and help him feel successful? How might she follow up later?

Next Ms. Flores passed around index cards while saying, *Todos miren a la maestra. Yo les voy a dar una tarjeta. En la parte de atrás, escribe tu nombre. Y entonces en el otro lado, está una línea. Vamos a escribir, "El elefante come _____."* *Ustedes tienen que escoger qué come.* [Everyone look at the teacher. I am going to give you a card. On the back, write your name. And then on the other side, there is a line. We are going to write, "The elephant eats _____." You have to choose what it eats.] She read the list on the board to them and laughed. Some of the students were talking. A student exclaimed, *¡Yo vi muchas Es! ¡Sí, Ms. Flores! ¡Ms. Flores!* [I see many *E*s! Yes!] The teacher circulated around the room, and said *¿Qué mesa va a trabajar más lindo? Me gusta la mesa _____.* [Which table is going to work the most nicely? I like the table _____.] All students were now quiet, writing. One asked, *¿Tú tienes que escoger qué come el elefante?* [You have to choose what the elephant eats?] We heard the first English by a student, who whispered to his neighbor, "Do you have an eraser? I wanted to pick . . ." We left while the students were working on this assignment.

STOPANDTHINK

What skills is Ms. Flores teaching or reinforcing in this lesson? What techniques does she use to make learning fun for students?

Transitions. We observed Ms. Flores's classroom again shortly before the winter break. The room looked great—it was very colorful, with lots of student work up on the walls. It was time for the two classes to switch. Ms. Flores said (in English), "Phew. That was a lot of work, wasn't it? But you did a terrific job!" She directed students to unfold their papers and then give them to the table captains. She said, "I'm going to see which table is ready first. One, two, three, four (in a quiet voice), five (in a very quiet voice). Very good. You know what? I have to go back to Spanish." She and the kids counted, *uno, dos, tres, cachumbambre!* Ms. Chaney came to the door, ready with her students to switch. Ms. Flores said that they were ready too. The classes changed places. Ms. Flores said to the next group, *Yo quiero una sorpresa. Yo quiero una sorpresa. Voy a contar*. [I want a surprise. I want a surprise. I am going to count.] She hid behind the door and counted. Then she looked in and the class was all quiet—she blew them kisses and they blew kisses back to her.

STOPANDTHINK

What do you notice about how Ms. Flores and Ms. Chaney transition from one class to the next?

"Sponge" Activity (Effective Time Filler). We next observed the classroom a few months later toward the end of the school day. When we entered the room, Ms. Flores was sitting at a kidney-shaped table on the side of the room with six students. Again we noted that she seemed happy, to be having fun, and to really enjoy her students. Other students were working in groups of two or three at various other tasks around the room, in centers. For example, two were playing with Legos, three were coloring, two were painting with watercolors, and two were playing a math board game. All seemed busy. The outside door was open, and two big fans were blowing. It was warm in the classroom, but not unbearable (apparently the air conditioner was not working). At 1:45 PM a timer went off and the teacher counted to ten slowly in Spanish while students scrambled to clean up and return to their seats. When she was done counting and the students were all in their seats, she said, *Yo veo a* _____ [I see _____] many times, each time saying a different student's name. She turned to us and said in English, "What a day, with no air conditioner!"

Then Ms. Flores asked the class in Spanish who wanted to play a game. She told them they had five minutes until it was time to go home. A few students called out names of games. Some students showed her the watercolor pictures they had painted. The teacher sang, *Me gusta Cristina, me gusta Lorenzo . . .* [I like . . .]. The students were now quiet again and she said in Spanish, "Now we are ready for the game." She wrote various numbers on the board, scattered and in random order. Students said them aloud, in unison, while she wrote them.

STOPANDTHINK

Effective teachers make good use of every instructional moment, even the four or five minutes at the end of the day before students are dismissed. What other "sponges" can you think of, to be used as students are entering class or when they finish an activity earlier than expected?

She announced, *¡Papa caliente!* [hot potato] and the students cheered. She threw a bean bag to Lorenzo first, while saying *papa caliente.* He caught it and then she said *el número uno.* He went to the board and crossed out the number one and everyone cheered. This continued (students clearly had played the game before and knew just what to do). When the teacher said a number (such as el número once), students chanted it while the student who had caught the bean bag walked up to the board. This seemed easy for students (all their answers were correct), and they were very engaged. The entire game lasted only about four minutes. Then the teacher turned out the light and turned it on again, saying that they would play the game again tomorrow. It was time to get ready to go home.

Calendar Time and Journal Writing. We observed the classroom again about a month later. Ms. Flores had written on the whiteboard: *Hoy es _____, 18 de abril del 2000. Yo veo _____.* [Today is _____, April 18, 2000. I see _____.] The students were supposed to read the sentences and say the words that went in the blanks when directed to do so by the teacher. The day of the week was *martes* (Tuesday). She called on Lorenzo first. He stood and looked at the board where she was pointing, but didn't say anything. (He should have said *Hoy.*) She moved on, asking another student. When it was time to write the day, she pointed to a list of the days of the week, also on the board. She pointed to each and asked students if the word was *martes* (the correct day of the week). All of this was conducted in Spanish. As she pointed to each day of the week (other than

> *When the teacher said a number (such as* el número once), *students chanted it while the student who had caught the bean bag walked up to the board. This seemed easy for students (all of their answers were correct), and they were very engaged. The entire game lasted only about four minutes.*

martes), the class said in unison, "No, no." She asked what letter *martes* started with. A student responded, *M*. So when she pointed to *miércoles* a few students incorrectly answered, "Yes." Then she pointed to the second letter in *miércoles,* and some students said, "No." When she finally pointed to *martes,* she had all of the students with her, and together they shouted *¡Sí!* and cheered. We were very impressed at how skilled she was at captivating them, even for something as mundane as this. She had them hanging on her every word.

Next Ms. Flores passed out students' journals—they were to write their names and copy what she had written on the board, filling in the blanks for the day of the week and something they could see. She circulated around the room, helping individual students. When she got to Ingrid, she whispered in Spanish, "Ingrid, I missed you a lot, where did you go?" Ingrid responded, "Honduras." She asked, "Did you enjoy yourself?" Ingrid responded, "*Sí.*" Brandon raised his hand and asked how to spell "Ms. Flores." She asked him what sound he heard first. He said, "M." She replied, "F," and wrote "Flores" on the board. She continued circulating around stamping finished journal entries with a star and then at 12:50 PM told the students that journal writing time was over. She appointed two students to collect the journals.

The class then got a little noisy, so she turned out the lights, and asked them to *fíjense* [pay attention]. She said that she knew that they were very *contentos* [happy] that week. She next demonstrated very awkward body movements, putting a leg way up in the air, asking how she looked. A student said, *Fea* [ugly]. She chided them to sit properly. Then she turned the lights back on.

Science Lesson. Ms. Flores told the class they were going to do something special and that she had a magic word. She said, with great suspense, *¡Científicos!* [Scientists!]. She asked what it meant. A student said, *Locos* [Crazy]. The teacher said, "No." Another student asked, *¿Mágicos?* [Magic?] "No." Other students guessed, and their guesses were not close. The teacher said that she was going to tell them. In Spanish she explained, "They are persons who do *experiments* (saying this last word with emphasis, after a slight pause to build suspense), like discovering medicine. They were the ones who observed that plants need water and sun to grow." The students seemed to be hanging on every word she said, enraptured. Ms. Flores told them they were going to be scientists (still in Spanish). She directed them to put on their thinking caps, special glasses, special gloves, and lab coats (in pantomime). A student said, *¡Y los pantalones!* [And the pants!] The teacher said that they did not need pants because they had the lab coats. Now they were going to say the magic word and they would become scientists, *¡Uno, dos, tres, cachachumbre!* She shook all over while saying this.

STOPANDTHINK

In what ways does the teacher get students' attention and hold it while teaching? What do you do to get your students' attention and maintain it? Can you think of additional ways to increase student involvement?

Then she said, "There are many intelligent and special scientists in this class." She said, *Me encanta Lorenzo.* [I love Lorenzo (praising how well he was paying attention).] She sent him to get a clothespin (part of her reward system). She put two glasses on each table. While she was doing this, a student said, *Yo quiero mi mamá.* [I want my mama.] Ms. Flores responded, *Yo también.* [Me too.] The students laughed. She told them not to touch the glasses or they would get contaminated. She asked if they knew what contaminated meant and explained it meant *sucio* [dirty]. Then she asked selected students to bring one of the cups from their table and go with her. Some of the remaining students guessed that these students would be getting water. Others said that they thought the students would be getting Sprite.

Concerns About Struggling Students. Both Ms. Chaney and Ms. Flores told us they believed the dual immersion model helped them distinguish between students who were struggling because of lack of proficiency in English or Spanish and students who were struggling in both languages and might need more intensive support because of possible learning disabilities, developmental disabilities, or an emotional disorder. They pointed out that it was easy for them to tell if a child was just having trouble learning in her new language but doing well in her more proficient language, because together they taught in both languages. Also, most of their students were progressing quite well, so they were able to compare how their few struggling students were doing in comparison with similar peers. They also noted that it was very beneficial to be able to talk with each other about their students and share insights and concerns. The two teachers met every day after school for this purpose.

> *Both Ms. Chaney and Ms. Flores said it was easy to tell if a child was just having trouble learning in her new language but doing well in her more proficient language, because together they taught in both languages.*

TEACHER'S VOICE

We asked Ms. Flores for her advice about working with students' families. She suggests taking the time to meet with parents as often as possible, especially when their child seems to be struggling. She recommends meeting with them formally at least once a month, so that parents can "come and see the progress of the child." She explains:

> At first, some of our parents are reluctant to accept that we are concerned about their child. As we work with them and we are very open with them, we explain that we are not attacking the child, that what we want to do is help. . . . We show them their work. We take that extra time, and as time passes they become more accepting to us and the situation. We also show them things they can do at home to help their child. For example, Lucas loves animals, and we were able to find a way to include animals in the letters. And the mother was really excited about that, because she saw the interest and the change in her child. He had been a totally negative child; everything that had to do with education was very hard for him. And when we found this area that he just loves—he loves animals—it just happened. We wanted to teach him the letters, and if we taught him the letters with an animal, he got it just like that.

CONCLUSION

In this chapter, we have provided glimpses of the bilingual instruction provided by two highly skilled kindergarten teachers, each with a different teaching style. They complement each other well and illustrate that not all effective instruction looks the same, but varies just as personalities vary. These teachers clearly were in tune with their students and very focused on making sure they were learning. They exemplify our understanding of "what works" in many ways. They incorporate the following techniques on a regular basis:

- Provide a welcoming, safe learning environment

- Are "with it," positive teachers with excellent classroom management

- Teach using creative, engaging, imaginative lessons that capture students' interest and hold their attention

- Use smooth transitions and do not waste time, but instead strive to make the most of every moment—for instance, by playing a quick game of hot potato to reinforce math skills in the last few minutes of class

- Sometimes teach students in small, flexible groups in which they could tailor instruction to meet students' needs

- Provide explicit instruction in letters and sounds

- Provide multiple and varied opportunities for practice

- Scaffold instruction so that students can feel successful and make progress toward learning target skills—for instance, by helping Freddie come up with a word that begins with *E*

- Assess students' learning on a continuous basis and keep track of what students know and need to learn, both in writing and in their heads—for instance, knowing that Isabel still needed to learn *J*

- Use thematic instruction to develop deep understanding—for instance, by connecting storybook reading with science instruction using *Chicka, Chicka, Boom, Boom; Jack and the Beanstalk;* learning the parts of a tree or plant; and growing bean plants

- Read appealing children's literature to students and engage them in meaningful discussions about the books

- Teach reading comprehension strategies—for instance, by asking students to predict what might happen next

- Teach and reinforce new vocabulary in English and Spanish using visual cues and multiple examples—for instance, by pantomiming dressing as *científicos* and doing an experiment like scientists or by labeling plant parts

- Build on students' prior knowledge

- Look for ways to connect with each child on an individual basis—for instance, by using animals to teach Lucas his letters

- Work closely with parents, especially when students show signs of struggling

STOPANDTHINK

Can you think of any other ways these teachers exemplified effective teaching? Which of these do you already do well? Which would you like to do more?

ACTIVITY

Role-play an after-school meeting between Ms. Chaney and Ms. Flores about Carlos, a student they are concerned about because he does not seem to be progressing in reading. Carlos speaks Spanish at home and is considered to be at a beginning to intermediate level in English. What kinds of information would they share about Carlos? What questions might they ask each other? What are the next steps they should take?

DISCUSSION QUESTIONS

1. What are Ms. Chaney's strengths as a teacher? What are Ms. Flores' strengths as a teacher? Are you more like Ms. Chaney or Ms. Flores? Why do you think so?

2. We have observed glimpses of Ms. Chaney's and Ms. Flores' reading instruction, but not everything they did. What stood out about their reading instruction? Did you notice that neither teacher used worksheets? In what other ways do you think they might have taught reading?

3. What do you think of Ms. Chaney's advice for working with parents? Have you also experienced resistance from parents when you explain that you are concerned about their child? What do you do to establish positive working relationships with your students' parents?

CHAPTER

3

BILINGUAL FIRST-GRADE INSTRUCTION

Michael Orosco and Janette K. Klingner

A SNAPSHOT OF THE CLASSROOM

Lucero is a Latina first-grade bilingual learner with sparkling dark eyes, long rib-boned braids, and a ready, friendly smile. Like her parents and the community all around her, she speaks Spanish. According to her teacher, Ms. Durcal, both her expressive and receptive native language skills are high. She is learning to read in Spanish while also acquiring oral English skills; the early literacy skills she is developing are beginning to transfer to English. She is an alert, active, and engaging first grader who is developing the oral language and emergent reading skills needed to be successful in school. It is still early in the year. Today Ms. Durcal is reading a passage to the class: *"Prietita estaba en la casa de la curandera"* [Prietita was at the house of the healer]. Lucero is sitting on the ABC rug

Note: Classroom observations in this chapter were conducted by Michael Orosco as part of his dissertation research. M. J. Orosco, *Response to intervention with Latino English language learners.* Unpublished doctoral dissertation, University of Colorado at Boulder, 2007. (ProQuest-CSA, LLC 072699).

in front of her, listening in rapt attention. When Ms. Durcal reads this sentence, Lucero's eyes widen and she raises her hand. Ms. Durcal calls on her and with excitement in her voice she shares: *"La curandera. ¡Mi abuela es una curandera en México! Ayuda a los enfermos."* [The healer. My grandmother is a healer in Mexico! She helps sick people.] Ms. Durcal responds that, yes, *curanderas* help sick people. Lucero smiles with pride. This is an important step in helping Lucero view herself as a learner and valued member of her class. It is also testament to the efforts her school is making to extend and elaborate upon her native language and connect it to her school experiences. Lucero is receiving bilingual instruction.

In this chapter we describe the bilingual teaching of Ms. Durcal, a first-grade teacher at Mi Piquito de Oro (MPO) Elementary. Ms. Durcal's classroom provides an oasis for her students—a haven with a warm, welcoming environment in which they can flourish. Inside her classroom these students are "thriving bilinguals." Unfortunately, in other classrooms in this very school, similar peers are seen as "limited" or "deficient" because they are not yet fully proficient in English and struggle with English reading. (See Orosco, 2007, for examples from classrooms in this same school where teachers did not provide English language learners with effective instruction—in English or Spanish—and saw them as deficient, lamenting that they "couldn't learn to read.") MPO does not have a formal bilingual program, though teachers can teach for part of the day in Spanish if they wish. Before we describe Ms. Durcal and her instruction, let us take a look at Mi Piquito de Oro Elementary School.

ABOUT MI PIQUITO DE ORO ELEMENTARY SCHOOL

MPO and its school district are situated in a working-class Midwestern suburb. As one teacher explained, "This used to be a working-class side of town; it personified the working middle class; now, because of outsourcing, it has become an immigrant-based community with immigrant-run businesses and labor. Now there are just *taquerias, tiendas,* and *llanteras* (taco shops, stores, and tire shops). There are no dreams here; there are just immigrants." The principal added that MPO used to be a white middle-class school, but over the past several years its student demographics shifted from "mainly white to mainly poor Latino English language learners." Another teacher said, "When I started here in the mid-1980s, it was a white working middle-class community. Now this has changed. I am not used to teaching these types of kids."

The school and its community preserve a kind of weary dignity, a toughness that comes from its new working-class immigrant population. As one drives into the community, one can begin to see the deteriorating and poorly maintained pre-1960s housing. There are fences to be mended, houses to be painted, and roofs to be shingled. Dogs run loose. Broken cars stand on homemade auto lifts made of cement blocks and plywood.

Driving up to the school, one can see that the brick building is starting to decay; there is no lawn, just brown patches of grass, and the parking lot has potholes. The playground equipment does not resemble the modern ecological playscapes found in newer schools in the district; its playground is made of steel beams and rocks. When asked why the school had not gotten a new playground, the custodian replied, "Why? So they can break it?" Physically, the school building and the classrooms show their forty-five years of age. The walls in the classroom are starting to crack, the plumbing makes noise, the air conditioning and heating ventilation system rattles as children try to read, the rugs give off a smell like wet puppies, and the rooms are too small for all of MPO's student inhabitants. The principal commented, "This school is long overdue for a remake." This is Kozol's (1991) *Savage Inequalities.*

Nevertheless, teachers and students do what they can to make this a school. Posters and student work hang from the plumbing and the ventilation system. Backpacks, books bags, and other materials rest on top of the heater, because there is little space elsewhere. Teachers and students busily carry out the work of the day. This school's treasures are its beautiful bilingual children, eager and ready to learn, and their families.

MPO has forty-three total staff members, including one principal and twenty-one teachers. The average years of teaching experience at the school is nine years. The demographics of the population are 14 percent white, 1 percent African American and Asian American, and 85 percent Latino students. Eighty percent of the Latino students are considered English language learners (and their first language is Spanish). Most of the Latino students' families are from Mexico.

MPO's language policy. Although neither the school nor its district has an official language policy, the dominant language of instruction at MPO is English. MPO mostly operates an English as a second language (ESL) immersion program that provides both pull-out and in-class ESL services. In Ms. Durcal's class, students' native language (Spanish) is used with ESL pull-out to support literacy development, as all learners are Spanish-dominant and emergent bilinguals in the process of acquiring English.

Student Assessment. All students are required to take the mandated state and local assessments, unless they are exempt from testing due to state or district recommendations. In addition, teachers use a Developmental Reading Assessment (DRA), progress monitoring using the Dynamic Indicators of Basic Early Literacy

Skills (DIBELS) and running records. In addition, the students are assessed with the Woodcock-Muñoz Language Survey (Revised), an oral language proficiency assessment tool in both English and Spanish.

Response to Intervention (RTI). MPO is implementing RTI for the first time. Tier 1 literacy instruction is provided in ninety-minute blocks. The amount of time spent on various instructional reading components varies. For example, phonemic awareness instruction is usually done at the start of the class and usually lasts five to fifteen minutes, depending on the teacher. Tier 2 literacy instruction supplements the ninety-minute reading block and is provided in small groups; sessions last fifteen to thirty minutes, depending on the content being provided. Tier 3 is special education.

MS. DURCAL'S INSTRUCTIONAL PHILOSOPHY

Ms. Durcal is a veteran elementary bilingual teacher with twenty years of experience. She has a masters degree in bilingual elementary education with bilingual and reading endorsements. She teaches a class that is full of bilingual Latino children. "I fell in love with Mexico in my twenties—spent time there learning the culture and language." She empathizes with her students: "I understand where these children are coming from. These kids and their families have to deal with the hardships of life. Many are undocumented, encounter violence and neglect, and have to deal with America's greed and materialism." She is also an advocate. During RTI problem-solving meetings, she is vocal about bilingual learners' need for adequate funding, well-trained teachers, appropriate assessments and instructional methods, and other resources from MPO's district administrators. She believes that "federal and state legislation failed to address the cultural and linguistic needs of [her] bilingual learners by failing to enforce civil rights policies such as *Lau* v. *Nichols*." She expresses dismay about what she calls "political attacks on English language learner communities such as anti-immigrant, English-only, and antibilingual education initiatives," adding, "we can behave better."

Beliefs About Her Students' Families. Ms. Durcal visits her students' homes and speaks with families in Spanish to get to know them and talk about their life experiences. She emphasizes the importance of working with parents and other family members as valued partners, holding up a book called *Con Respeto* by Guadalupe Valdés (1996), and saying, "If you do not understand this, you are not going to understand how to teach these kids. Most of my students' parents come from Mexico. I explain to them that their children are learning two languages. I tell them that English is developing, and because of this it is important for them not only to make them speak English, but also to maintain their Spanish at home. I tell the parents this is a big part of who they are and that they need to be involved." Before and after school, she stands outside her classroom door greeting parents and welcoming them to the school, saying, *"Siempre estoy aquí para servirles"* ("I am always here to serve you").

Ms. Durcal makes an effort to draw upon their cultural capital by asking parents and grandparents to read to their kids in Spanish. She understands that this is important, whether their children are first learning to read in English or Spanish. However, she recognizes that not all parents have time to do this because, as she explains, "Some of these parents live complex lives, and this requires them to work two jobs." She encourages siblings and other relatives to read with students as well.

> *Ms. Durcal makes an effort to draw upon their cultural capital by asking parents and grandparents to read to their kids in Spanish.*

Parents and grandparents sometimes participate in classroom activities to help address cultural and linguistic differences. She believes that by encouraging parents and other family members to come into her classroom, they can learn about what is going on in their children's school life, and at the same time she can keep her students further engaged and motivated by having them visit the classroom and share their areas of expertise, or "funds of knowledge" (Moll, Armanti, Neff, & Gonzalez, 1992).

Classroom Management. Ms. Durcal spends little time on behavior and a lot of time on instruction. She believes that the best way to keep children engaged is to provide them with interesting, meaningful instruction at their level. Her classroom is like a family, where students work together and support one another. When students misbehave, whether during small- or large-group instruction or independent activities, Ms. Durcal pauses, walks past them, or simply touches a shoulder. She says nothing, but students understand her intent. At other times she calmly says, *"Niños, necesito que estén atentos a su tarea"* [Students, I need you to pay attention to your work]. Expectations are clear, and students are learning to regulate themselves.

Ms. Durcal's Classroom

Ms. Durcal's classroom is appealing and engaging, decorated with a southwestern personal touch. Colorful potted flowers, student art, rugs, and posters adorn the room. Cozy cushioned reading corners invite students to curl up with a good book. She shares: "I do not believe in basic bulletin boards or posters that are not educationally relevant. You will not see any Garfield posters here, but a very colorful classroom with bulletin boards that feature children's work, a lot of print, a lot of Spanish." As you enter the classroom, a sign states "*Quien sabe dos lenguas vale por dos* [One who knows two languages is worth two people]."

Ms. Durcal has created a room with ample space for materials and supplies. Her cozy reading corner is encompassed by mini-bookshelves to give the children easy access to books and less time "looking for books, more time for reading." Student desks are centered in the middle of the class and grouped in fours so that students can work together. Ms. Durcal has a small desk at the back of the class, next to the student desks. She

> *"You will not see any Garfield posters here, but a very colorful classroom with bulletin boards that feature children's work, a lot of print, a lot of Spanish."*

explains, "My desk placement allows me to be within reach of a student pretty quickly. I can see my students at all times, which motivates them to learn and reduces problem behavior."

The classroom is set up for cooperative learning. Ms. Durcal has clearly designated spaces for large- and small-group activities. Two medium tables and one large kidney-shaped table are set up for cooperative projects. Behind each table are word walls labeled *Cultivando Palabras* (Cultivating Words), *Palabras Compuestas* (Compound Words), *Prefijos* (Prefixes), *Sufijos* (Suffixes), and *Ráices* (Roots). Concept maps relate to daily instruction or weekly themes, and poster boards provide ideas. Ms. Durcal has created a classroom that enables her to differentiate instruction to meet her students' diverse needs.

Ms. Durcal's Reading Instruction

Ms. Durcal provides explicit native language instruction merged within a cooperative learning structure. She breaks down her instructional tasks into small steps, constantly probing to verify that students are understanding her instruction, administering frequent feedback, providing modeling (such as pictures, diagrams, and visuals), and always asking questions as comprehension checks. With a simple "*¿Comprenden?*" [Do you understand?] and a pause to provide some think time, she monitors their understanding. If there is very little student feedback, she goes back and modifies instruction and then repeats this process. In this way she differentiates instruction. She then reinforces her instruction through small-group and peer-assisted collaborative activities. She calls herself an "interactive-based primary teacher. I use the cooperative reading cycle, day in and day out." Her classroom includes a blend of emerging, beginning, and accelerated bilingual learners. She provides daily oral language opportunities, small-group, and individualized literacy activities (guided and independent practice), and structured small-group strategic reading instruction to foster reading comprehension skills.

Small groups in Ms. Durcal's class are sometimes structured so that students can make choices, depending on the activity. She explains: "My students need to learn how to make good choices. This is why at times I allow them to choose their own groups for certain activities. It helps to produce strong regulation skills. At other times, I have to make the choices because they need specialized small-group differentiated instruction." Choices depend on previous activities relevant to students' reading levels and learning needs. For example, if the reader is emerging or beginning, small-group activities focus on phonemic awareness, sight word recognition, and word study. When working independently, students can choose from different activities that focus on writing, concepts of print, letter-sound correspondence (such as matching letters with objects beginning with the same sounds), or cut-up sentences that need to be put in the right order and read. Independent reading involves leveled readers with various books so that students have choices at their independent reading levels. They read by themselves and also to each other or a volunteer (a parent or someone from the community).

Ms. Durcal's instruction is conducted in Spanish; her standards-based hybrid reading curriculum is theme-related and approved by the school district. Excerpts of this curriculum follow. The first example shows an introductory lesson with the entire class. The second excerpt demonstrates how Ms. Durcal conducts a guided reading lesson. The next two excerpts show what students do as follow-up activities while she works with another guided reading group; they answer comprehension questions or read words together in a reading center. The final excerpt shows another guided reading lesson. Ms. Durcal calls her guided reading lessons the "heart of my reading program." Examples are provided first in Spanish (as they actually took place in the classroom), with English translations following.

Warm-Up, Student Discussion, and Preparation for the Day (Whole Class, for Approximately Fifteen Minutes). Ms. Durcal waits calmly until everyone is seated and quiet on the ABC rug. The students understand her quietness cue. She always begins her sessions with a warm-up activity that connects to the daily lesson. In today's activity, she activates their prior knowledge and helps them connect to their lives the story they will be reading. This creates interest in the story and helps with their comprehension. Ms. Durcal uncovers a concept map with the word *fotos* [photos] in the middle on a chart paper board.

Ms. Durcal:	*¿Alguien en la clase se ha tomado fotos antes?*
Lupe:	*Mi sobrina tuvo una quinciñera el sábado y tomamos bastante fotos.*
Ms. Durcal:	[writes the word *quinceañera* and connects it to the word *fotos.*] *Lupe, ¿tomaron fotos con vestidos lindos?*
Lupe:	*Si estaban hermosos.* [Some of the students are not paying attention.]
Ms. Durcal:	[Pauses, waits quietly; students understand this cue, put their hands in their laps, and begin to pay attention.] *¿Quién más?*
Jaime:	*Cuando tuve mi cumpleaños, tomamos fotos.*
Ms. Durcal:	[writes the word *cumpleaños* and connects it to the word *fotos.*] *¿Tomaron fotos de tu pastel?*
Jaime:	[smiling] *Sí.*
Rocky:	*El año pasado tomamos fotos al final del año escolar.*
Ms. Durcal:	*¡Qué bien! ¿Les gusta cómo aparecieron en ellas? ¿A quién no le gusta?*
Ms. Durcal:	[Calls on a few more students and connects their ideas to the term *fotos.*] *Qué bien! Ahora tenemos bastantes temas para fotos. Las fotos son para recordar los momentos más importantes en nuestras vidas.*

English Translation

Ms. Durcal:	Who in the class has taken photos before?
Lupe:	My cousin had her *quinceañera* (party to celebrate her fifteenth birthday; a coming-of-age party) on Saturday, and we took lots of photos.
Ms. Durcal:	[Writes the word *quinceañera* and connects it to the word *fotos.*] Lupe, did you take photos of pretty dresses?
Lupe:	Yes, they were beautiful. [Some of the students are not paying attention.]
Ms. Durcal:	[Pauses, waits quietly; students understand this cue, put their hands in their laps, and begin to pay attention.] Who else?

Jaime:	When I had my birthday party, we took photos.
Ms. Durcal:	[Writes the word *cumpleaños* (birthday) and connects it to the word *fotos.*] Did you take pictures of your cake?
Jaime:	[smiling] Yes.
Rocky:	This last year we took pictures of the end of the school year.
Ms. Durcal:	Good! Did you like how you looked in the photos? Who didn't?
Ms. Durcal:	[Calls on a few more students and connects their ideas to the term *fotos.*] Good, now we have enough ideas about photos. Photos help us remember important moments in our lives.

STOPANDTHINK

How has Ms. Durcal connected the concept of *fotos* to the children's lives?

Second part of warm-activity:

Ms. Durcal:	[holding up a book] *Tengo un libro con el título* La foto del salón (Sayers-Ward, 2005). *¿Qué significa este título?* [She asks them to raise their hands and asks one student to answer her question.]
Horacio:	*Parece que es como un salón de clase con niños y un niño está tomando una foto con una cámara.*
Ms. Durcal:	[Looks at the book title and then observes students to see if they understand.] *Ahora vamos a repasar unos sonidos, letras, y palabras que van a necesitar para leer este cuento. Recuerdan estos sonidos de ayer: ¡FI FA FO FU FE! Repitan por favor.*
Students:	*¡FI FA FO FU FE!*
Ms. Durcal:	*Fila Fabuloso Famosos Cámara.*
Students:	*Fila Fabuloso Famosos Cámara.*
Ms. Durcal:	*Fifi fotógrafo formen vez.*
Students:	*Fifi fotógrafo formen vez.*

Ms. Durcal: *Falta fugó fenomenal fin.* [Students repeat this, appearing engaged and motivated.]

Ms. Durcal: *Quiero explicarles que a veces van a mirar palabras que no son muy comunes. Un ejemplo es palabras que llevan la letra Z. Esto significa que la palabra tiene una letra como una colita al final de las sílabas.*

Ms. Durcal: [reading] *ve, ve, z, vez. Pepe no pudo tomar la foto del salón la primera vez.* [She has students repeat this.]

English Translation

Ms. Durcal: [holding up a book] I have a book titled *The Classroom Photo*. What does this title mean? [She asks them to raise their hands and asks one student to answer her question.]

Horatio: It looks like a classroom with kids.

Ms. Durcal: [Looks at the book title and then observes students to see if they understand.] Now we are going to work on our letters, sounds, and words for today's story. Do you remember these sounds? *FI FA FO FU FE!* Repeat, please.

Students: *FI FA FO FU FE!*

Ms. Durcal: *Fila Fabuloso Famosos Cámara.*

Students: *Fila Fabuloso Famosos Cámara.*

Ms. Durcal: *Fifi fótografo formen vez.*

Students: *Fifi fótografo formen vez.*

Ms. Durcal: *Falta fugó fenomenal fin.* [Students repeat this, appearing engaged and motivated.]

Ms. Durcal: I want to explain to you that at times you are going to see words that are not very common. An example of this is words that have the letter *Z* at the end. This means that the word has a letter like a little tail at the end of the syllables.

Ms. Durcal: [reading] *ve, ve, z, vez.* Pepe could not take a classroom photo the first time *[primera vez]* in class. [She has students repeat this.]

Ms. Durcal assigns students to small-group reading activities. Some students work collaboratively in groups while she works with a guided reading group.

Guided Reading Group (Fifteen to Twenty Minutes). The following guided reading lesson is with a group of five first-grade Latino English language learners. These children are reading at the 1.5 to 1.8 level and have already mastered concepts of print and letter sounds and syllables, and have reached a somewhat independent reading level for mid-first-grade. The reading text, *La Foto del Salon*, was appropriate for this reading level (less than 90 percent reading accuracy).

Ms. Durcal:	*Ahora vamos a hacer nuestra guía de lectura sobre lo que leímos ayer.* [Holding up *La foto del salón.* Students each have their own book.]
Ms. Durcal:	*¿Quién quiere ir primero?* [There is no hesitation; all the students volunteer. They are eager to read.]
Luis:	[reading] *Es vier . . . nes y Dani está muy con . . . ten.to por . . . que lo han nom . . . brado el fotó . . . grafo oficial de la escuela.* [Some pauses in the fluency; while he is reading, the other students follow along in their books.]
Ms. Durcal:	*Luisito, ¿puedes leer el pasaje otra vez?, me encanta como lees.* [Luis rereads passage more fluently.]
Ms. Durcal:	*¡Muy bien! ¿Quién sigue?*
Donaldo:	*Dani es el fotógrafo para el boletín. ¡Miren! Tengo esta cámara para tomar fotos, dice Dani. Tómanos una foto, dice la señorita Peña. Sí, formen una fila, dice Dani.*
Ms. Durcal:	*¿Así se lee una frase que tiene punto de exclamación?* [Students look at her with hesitation; they do not know what she means.] *¿Alguien nos puede ayudar?* [Nobody volunteers.] *¡Ay! está bien. Un punto de exclamación es que lees esa frase con emócion. Por ejemplo,* ¡Miren! [She models this word by saying it with a strong emphasis.]
Ms. Durcal:	*¿Comprenden?* [She asks Donald to reread the sentence with expression.] *¿Qué es* un boletín? [Students pause for some time; no one knows the answer.] *Un boletín es como un periódico de escuela. Les da información sobre algo importante. ¿Comprenden?*
Luis:	*Sí. Mi papá lee un periódico de noticias.*
Ms. Durcal:	*Muy bien. Eso es una forma de boletín. Anna, por favor, sigue.*

Anna: *Todos los niños están felices porque mo . . . .stra . . .rán* [Ms. Durcal helps Anna pronounce this word; Anna continues] *la foto del primer grado en el pa.si.llo prin.ci.pal de la escuela.*

Ms. Durcal: *¿La palabra* mostrarán—*qué significa?* [Students pause; no answer.]

Ms. Durcal: *La palabra* mostrarán *significa que van a demostrar o enseñar. Como lo que estoy haciendo ahora. Cuando ustedes me muestran algo es que ya lo saben y me están enseñando. ¿Comprenden?* [She looks around for comprehension checks. Students nod. Everybody seems to understand.] *Muy bien.*

Luis: [reading] *¿Estamos todos para la foto? pregunta Dani. ¡Espera! Falta Ofelia, dice la señorita Peña. Paco dice: ¡Ofelia se fugó! ¡Ofelia! ¡Ofelia! gritan los niños.* [Luis reads this passage with emphasis; he remembers what the teacher said about *el punto de exclamación.*]

Lupita: [reading] *Dani está un poco impaciente porque lo que más desea es tomar la foto de su grupo. ¿Qué pasa?¡Ofelia, apúrate para la foto! grita Dani. Dani está enfadado. La fila de niños se rompe. Los niños buscan a Ofelia.*

Donaldo: [reading] *Paco, Trini y Dani buscan a Ofelia por toda la escuela. Los niños buscan a Ofelia en el sótano. De pronto: Pif, pif. ¡Oh, oh! ¿Qué es eso? pregunta Paco.*

Luis: [reading] *No sé, dice Trini asustada. Los niños caminan temerosos buscando a su amiga. Otra vez: Pif, pif. ¿Será Ofelia? preguntan todos. Los niños buscan en el fondo del sótano.*

Ms. Durcal: *¿Qué es este* Pif Pif? [Students do not know the answer.] *Vamos a ver.*

Anna: *Allí se llevan una sorpresa. ¿Qué encuentran? ¡Ofelia, por fin! Grita Trini. Hola, amigos. Estos son los gatitos de Fifí dice Ofelia.¿Fifí? preguntan los niños. Sí, Fifí es la gata de la escuela, responde Ofelia. Ofelia presenta a los niños a la gata Fifí, quien está recostada en sus faldas.*

Ms. Durcal: *Sigue, Horacio.*

Horacio: *Ellos tienen cur.io.si.dad de saber lo que o . . . cu . . . rrió. ¿Qué pasó, Ofelia? pregunta Trini. ¿Por qué no fuiste a tomarte la foto? Pregunta Dani. Es que Fifí está ago . . . ta . . . da porque tuvo gatitos. ¡Miren sus gatitos! dice Ofelia.*

Ms. Durcal: *Niños, vamos a leer ese pasaje otro vez juntos.* [They read it again.]

Ms. Durcal: *La palabra* curiosidad—*qué significa?* [Students look perplexed.] *Vamos al pasaje otra vez, cuando tienen batalla con alguna palabra tienen que buscar ayuda en el contexto. Leen la oración sin la palabra.* [reading the sentence with the word *curiosidad*] *Ellos tienen . . . de saber lo que o . . . cu . . . rrió. Piensen en la palabra que tendría sentido en ese lugar.* [Pauses, giving students think time.]

Donaldo: *Ellos tienen . . . interés de saber lo que occurió.*

Ms. Durcal: *¿Cómo supiste que curiosidad era como tener interés?*

Donaldo: *Cuando quiero saber de algo . . . es como tener interés o ganas de saber algo.*

Ms. Durcal: *¿Miraron lo que hizo Donaldo? Conectó el contexto de la frase para resolver una palabra desconocida. ¡Muy bien, Donaldo! Y otras veces si no pueden usar esta estrategia pueden pedir ayuda.*

Ms. Durcal: *Ahora leemos juntos, repitan lo que leo.* [Reading] *Ofelia cuenta a los niños que ella descubrió que la gata Fifí tuvo gatitos esa mañana y que fue a conocerlos. ¡Tomemos la foto con Fifí y sus gatitos! dice Dani. ¡Fenomenal! dice Ofelia. Todos posan para la foto. ¡Fabuloso! Fifí y sus gatitos serán famosos dicen todos. El fin.*

English Translation

Ms. Durcal: Now we are going to do guided reading. [She holds up *The Classroom Picture*. Students each have their own book.]

Ms. Durcal: Who would like to go first? [There is no hesitation; all the students volunteer. They are eager to read.]

Luis: [reading] It is Friday and Dani is happy because he has been named the school's photographer. [Some pauses in the fluency. While he is reading, the other students follow along in their books.]

Ms. Durcal: Luisito, can you read the passage again? I love how you read. [Luis rereads the passage more fluently.]

Ms. Durcal: Very good! Who wants to continue?

Donaldo: [reading] Dani is the official photographer for the school bulletin. Look! I have this camera to take pictures. Let's take a picture, says Ms. Peña. Please form a line, says Dani. [He reads without much expression.]

Ms. Durcal: How do we read a passage with an exclamation point? [Students look at her with hesitation; they do not know what she means.] Can someone help us? [Nobody volunteers.] That's okay. An exclamation point means you read a passage with emotion. For example, *Look!* [She models this word by saying it with a strong emphasis.] Understand? [She asks Donald to reread the sentence with expression.]

Ms. Durcal: What is a bulletin? [She is asking questions about the story now. Students pause for some time; no one knows the answer.] A bulletin is a newspaper about the school. It gives you important information about something. Understand? [Students nod their head in understanding.]

Luis: Yes. My father reads a newspaper for the news.

Ms. Durcal: Very good. A newspaper is like a bulletin. Anna, please continue.

Anna: [reading] All the children are happy because they are going to display . . . [Anna struggles to pronounce *display;* Ms. Durcal helps her.] the photo of the first grade in the main hallway of the school.

Ms. Durcal: What does the word *display* mean? [The students pause; no answer.]

Ms. Durcal: The word *display* means that they are going to demonstrate or show it. Like what I am doing now. When you show me something, it means you already know it and you are showing me. Understand? [She looks around to check comprehension; students nod; everyone seems to understand.] Very good.

Luis: [reading] Is everyone ready for the picture? asks Dani. Wait, Ofelia is missing! says Ms. Peña. Paco says: Ofelia ran away! Ofelia! Ofelia! the children shout. [Luis reads this passage with emphasis; he remembers what the teacher taught him about the exclamation point.]

Lupita: [reading] Dani is impatient because he wants to take the picture of the class. What's wrong? Ofelia, hurry for the photo! yells Dani. Dani is furious. The students in line get out of place. The students are looking for Ofelia.

Donaldo: [reading] Paco, Trini, and Dani look for Ofelia throughout the school. They look for her in the basement, hurriedly: Pif, pif. Oh, oh! Who's there? asks Paco.

Luis: [reading] I do not know, says Trini, surprised. Once again: Pif, pif. Is it Ofelia? they ask.

Ms. Durcal: What is this *Pif Pif*? [Students do not know the answer.] Let's see.

Anna: [reading] There's a surprise. Who did they find? Ofelia, at last! yells Trini. Hello, friends. Are these Ofelia's kittens? ask the children. Yes, Fifí is the school's cat, Ofelia says. Ofelia shows the children the cat resting on her skirt.

Ms. Durcal: Continue, Horacio.

Horacio: They were curious to know what had happened. What happened, Ofelia? Trini asks. Why didn't you go to take the photo? asks Dani. It's because Fifí was exhausted. Look at her kittens! says Ofelia.

Ms. Durcal: Children, let's read that passage again together. [They read it again.]

Ms. Durcal: What does the word *curious* mean? [Students look perplexed.]

Ms. Durcal: Let's read the passage again. When we don't understand a word, we need to look for help in the context. Read the sentence again without the word.

Ms. Durcal: [reading] They were _____ to know what had happened. Think about what word make sense in this place. [She pauses, giving students think time.]

Donaldo: They were interested to know what had happened.

Ms. Durcal: So you suppose that curiosity is like having interest?

Donaldo: When I want to know something, it is like I have interest or a desire to know something.

Ms. Durcal: Look at what Donaldo did. He used the context to figure out the meaning of an unknown word. Very good, Donaldo! And if at other times you cannot use this strategy, you can ask for help.

Ms. Durcal: Now let's read together. Repeat what I read: Ofelia tells the children how she discovered that the cat Fifí had kittens this morning and that she went to get to know them. Let's take a photo with Fifí and her kittens! says Dani. Phenomenal! says Ofelia. Everyone poses for the photo. Fabulous! Fifí and her kittens will be famous! everyone says. The end.

STOPANDTHINK

In this fifteen-minute activity, Ms. Durcal provided small-group reading instruction that used various reading supports. What were some of these supports? How did Ms. Durcal use guided reading as way to encourage good readers? Are there other ways she might have reinforced reading skills? Would you do anything differently if you were teaching this lesson? Explain.

Follow-Up Activity. Once Ms. Durcal and her students have finished reading their story, she tells them that next, in their groups, they will be answering comprehension questions about the story. She uncovers the following questions clearly written on a whiteboard near the guided reading table:

¿Quién es el fotógrafo encargado de sacar la foto del salón? [Who is in charge of taking the classroom picture?]

¿Por qué se rompió la fila de los niños antes de tomar la foto? [Why did the children get out of line before taking the picture?]

¿Por qué se fue Ofelia al fondo del sótano? [Why did Ofelia go to the basement?]

¿Cómo se harían famosos Fifí y sus gatitos? [Why were Fifí and her kitten going to become famous?]

She asks the students to read the questions. She then clarifies the questions with them and asks them to return to their desks and answer them in their journals. She tells them that they can work on the questions collaboratively and that they will go over these questions the next time they meet.

She tells them they can work on the questions collaboratively, and they will go over these questions next time they meet.

STOPANDTHINK

What different types of comprehension questions does Ms. Durcal ask? In what ways does she focus on reading comprehension?

Practicing Words from La foto del salon *in a Reading Center.* While Ms. Durcal works with a guided reading group, other students work collaboratively in small groups in *los centros de leer* (reading centers). The following excerpt is from what she calls a *palabras de vista centro* (sight word center) with four students. She has made two sets of flash cards; one side has the target syllable, and the other side has a word that corresponds to this syllable. In this observation, she has made twelve flash cards with the *FI FA FO FU FE* syllables with words (*fila, Fifí, falta, fondo, fabuloso, fotógrafo, fugó, fotos, famosos, formen, fenomenal, fin*). These words reinforce words from the story students are reading in their guided reading groups. Students practice in pairs.

Diego: [holds up a card with the syllable *Fi* and shows it to Dora.]

Dora: [sounding it out with emphasis] *F . . . F . . . Fi.*

Diego: [flipping the card over and showing Dora the word] *Fila.*

Dora: [pausing, then stretching it] *Fi. . .Fi. . .Fi. . .la. . .Fila.*

Diego: [holding up another card] *Fa.*

Dora: *F. . .F. . .Fa.*

Diego: [flipping the card over] *Fabuloso.*

Dora: [reading with emphasis] *F. . .F. . .Fa. . .bu. . .lo. . .so. . .Fabuloso.*

Diego: [holding up the next card] *Fe.*

Dora: [hesitating] F. . .F. . .F. . .

Diego: [assisting her] *F. . .F. . .Fe.*

Dora: *F. . .F. . .Fe.*

Diego: [flipping the card over] *Fenomenal.*

Dora: [looks perplexed]

Diego: [assists by stretching the word] *F. . .F. . .Fe. . .Fe. . .no..me. . .nal.*

Dora: *F. . .F. . .F. . .Fe. . .Fe. . .Fe. . .no..me. . .nal, Fenomenal.*

Diego: *Cambiamos* [they switch places].

Students stayed on task and were able to assist each other when one struggled.

STOPANDTHINK

Which basic reading skills does Ms. Durcal address? How do you think Ms. Durcal may have prepared students to work together in centers in this way?

Guided Reading Group (Fifteen to Twenty Minutes). The following guided reading observation takes place with another group of five first-grade Latino English language learners from a little earlier in the year. This group is seated at a round table where guided reading is conducted. These children are reading at a 1.2 to 1.5 reading level.

Ms. Durcal:	*Hoy vamos a leer un libro que se llama* Tom es valiente. *¿Qué piensan sobre la palabra* valiente? [She is trying to activate prior knowledge. She pauses and realizes they may not recognize the word.] *Está bien. ¿Alguien alguna vez ha tenido miedo de algo?*
Students:	*Sí.*
Ms. Durcal:	*¿Alguien puede levantar la mano, para decirme a qué le tiene miedo?*
Olga:	*Yo tengo miedo de los perros. No me gustan.*
Ms. Durcal:	*No es nada malo tener miedo de los perros. A mí no me gustan los gatos. ¿Quién más tiene miedo de algo?*
Celia:	*Yo tengo miedo en la noche cuando me duermo.*
Ms. Durcal:	*Ah, tienes miedo de la oscuridad.* Oscuridad *es otra palabra para la noche.*
Ms. Durcal:	*Saben que todos tenemos miedo de algo. Ahora la palabra* valiente [pointing to title page] *significa no tener miedo de nada.*
Ms. Durcal:	*Ahora vamos a leer* Tom es valiente. [Title page has a picture of Tom's mom putting a bandage on his knee. Ms. Durcal directs Damaso to read.]
Damaso:	*Tom fue a la tienda con su mamá* [picture of Tom walking to the store; Ms. Durcal asks Ramón to read].
Ramon:	*¡Tom! ¡Tom! ¡Fíjate por donde caminas! ¡Fíjate por donde caminas!* [picture of Tom crossing the street almost being struck by a motorcyclist].
Ms. Durcal:	[after a pause] *¿Se recuerdan como deben leer cuando miren el punto de exclamación en un párrafo?*
Damaso:	*Tenemos que . . . leer con e . . . .mo . . . ción.* [She asks Ramón to reread the passage with emphasis, and he does.]
Ms. Durcal:	*¡Muy bien!*
Damaso:	*Yo me recuerdo una vez cuando tuve que cruzar una carretera y me dio tanto miedo.*
Ms. Durcal:	*Pero, la cruzaste. ¡Que valiente!* [She directs Thalía to read.]

Thalía: [reading with emphasis] *¡Oh! ¡Oh! ¡Oh!* [picture of Tom getting off the road quickly and stumbling onto the sidewalk]. *Tom lloró y lloró* [picture of Tom on the sidewalk clutching his left knee, crying in pain.]

Olga: *Tom se fue a casa. Mirá, mamá—estoy sangrando. ¡Oh, Tom! dijo la mamá.* [picture of Tom running home and mom waiting on the doorstep with open arms].

Ms. Durcal: *¿Qué significa la palabra* sangrando? [Olga, Celia, and Damaso raise their hands; she asks Olga to answer.]

Olga: *Es cuando te cortas con algo picoso y te sale sangre.*

Ms. Durcal: [smiling] *¿Te cortas con algo afilado?* [Olga looks perplexed.]

Ms. Durcal: *La palabra* afilado *es más apropiada para decir que* picoso. *Por ejemplo, el chile es picoso.* [She prompts Celia to read.]

Celia: *Aquí tienes, dijo la mamá. Eres valiente* [picture of mom applying a bandage to Tom's knee]. *Tom fue al mercado. ¡Mira! dijo. ¡Mírame!* [picture of Tom at the store showing his bandage to people].

Mrs. Durcal: *El fin.*

English Translation

Ms. Durcal: Today we are going to read a book called *Tom Is Brave.* What do you think the work *brave* means? [She is trying to activate prior knowledge. She pauses and realizes they may not recognize the word.] That's okay. Has anyone ever been afraid of something?

Students: Yes.

Ms. Durcal: Does anyone want to raise their hand and tell me if they are afraid of something?

Olga: I am afraid of dogs.

Ms. Durcal: There is nothing wrong with being afraid of dogs. I do not like cats. Who else is afraid of something?

Celia: I am afraid of the night when I go to sleep.

Ms. Durcal:	Oh, you are afraid of the dark. *Dark* is another word for night. We all are afraid of something. Now the word *brave* [pointing to title page] means *not* being afraid of something.
Ms. Durcal:	Now we are going to read *Tom Is Brave*. [Title page shows a picture of Tom with his mom putting a bandage on his knee. Ms. Durcal directs Damaso to read.]
Damaso:	[reading] Tom went to the store with his mom [picture of Tom walking to the store; Ms. Durcal asks Ramón to read.]
Ramón:	[reading] Tom! Tom! Watch where you are walking! Watch where you are walking! [picture of Tom crossing the street almost being struck by a motorcyclist].
Ms. Durcal:	[after a pause] Do you remember how to read a passage when you see the exclamation point?
Damaso:	We have to read with excitement. [She then asks Ramón to reread the passage with emphasis, and he does.]
Ms. Durcal:	Very good!
Damaso:	I remember when I had to cross a highway and I was really afraid.
Ms. Durcal:	But you crossed it. You were so brave! [She then directs Thalía to read.]
Thalía:	[reading with emphasis] Oh! Oh! Oh! [picture of Tom getting off the road quickly and stumbling onto the sidewalk]. Tom cried and cried. [Picture of Tom on the sidewalk clutching his left knee, crying in pain.]
Olga:	[reading] Tom went to his house. Momma, Momma, I am bleeding. Oh, Tom! said his mom [picture of Tom running home and mom waiting on the doorstep with open arms].
Mrs. Durcal:	What does *bleeding* mean? [Olga, Celia, and Damaso raise their hands; she asks Olga to answer.]
Olga:	It is when you cut yourself with something pointy and blood comes out.

Ms. Durcal: [smiling] Have you ever cut yourself with something sharp? [Olga looks perplexed.] The word *sharp* is more appropriate than *pointy*. For example, chile is sharp (*picoso*). [She asks Celia to read.]

Celia: Here you go, said the mother. You are brave [picture of mother applying a bandage to Tom's knee]. Tom went to the market. Look! he said. Look! [Picture of Tom at the store showing his bandage to people.]

Ms. Durcal: The end.

Ms. Durcal provides this type of native language instruction on a daily basis. She builds on what her students already know and helps them feel confident that they can learn and be successful. Ms. Durcal is able to provide direct

She sees her students as bringing many assets to the task of learning, including their motivation to learn and their emerging bilingualism.

and explicit native language instruction that is culturally responsive and appropriate to students' levels of language development. She does not view her students from a deficit perspective; on the contrary, she sees them as bringing many assets to the task of learning, including their motivation to learn and their emerging bilingualism. If there is a deficit in her classroom, it is that she needs more bilingual materials. She explains, "The school is not providing me with many materials. I have to build my own libraries. This takes time and money."

CONCLUSION

The foundation for her successful reading pedagogy was a combination of her attitude, knowledge, and high-quality, culturally responsive primary language instruction.

As you look back on what you have learned about Ms. Durcal, think about the ways in which she was successful. Ms. Durcal, like many teachers, was familiar with her students' cultural and linguistic differences. However, she went a step further not only by acknowledging that these differences are important, but also by understanding that these differences form the substance of who her students are and what they bring with them to school. It is this recognition that forms the basis for culturally responsive pedagogy. With this background in mind, Ms. Durcal understands that her

TEACHER'S VOICE

When asked what she thinks the key is to providing high-quality instruction for Latino ELLs, Ms. Durcal explained that she believes that good instruction starts first with a positive attitude, then proceeds with understanding her students, and finally applying effective practices. During interviews she made it very clear that she views her students as ready and able to learn: "When I look at a child, I am careful not to stereotype that child. I try not to label him as a second language learner. I just see him as a child who comes to my classroom to learn." She voiced concerns that the public school system seems to be moving away from this focus, and she feels that many educators "look through their eyes with bias, prejudice, and the fear of not knowing how to teach these kids to read." Next she emphasized that she "understands where these children are coming from. . . . They vary in the amount of instruction they need for learning to read. All of my students come from different places in Mexico and because of this, they have had so many different learning experiences. However, I need to meet the diverse needs of my students." In the end, she believes that the foundation for her successful reading pedagogy is a combination of her attitude, knowledge, and high-quality, culturally responsive primary language instruction.

Latino students' cultural and linguistic knowledge affect their reading development through "unseen variables" such as self-perception, self-esteem, and motivation. By understanding these variables and combining this awareness with her knowledge of how to provide native language instruction, she was able to help her students build a strong foundation for their bilingual reading development. Quite simply, Ms. Durcal is able to challenge the belief that "home cultures and native languages sometimes get in the way of student learning not because of the nature of the home cultures or native languages themselves but rather because they do not conform to the way the schools define learning" (Nieto, 1999, p. 67). She regularly incorporates the following principles into her instruction:

- Provides a warm, safe, nurturing learning environment

- Has high expectations of her students

- Is in tune with her students and understands their strengths as well as their needs

- Checks for understanding frequently

- Helps students connect what they are learning with their prior knowledge

- Focuses on vocabulary development and reading comprehension

- Develops partnerships with parents and other family members, visiting their homes and inviting them into the classroom

- Provides students with explicit instruction in small groups at their level

- Makes sure students have frequent opportunities to read engaging books at their level

- Provides students with choices to help them become self-regulated learners

- Assigns meaningful guided and independent practice activities

STOPANDTHINK

Can you think of other principles or practices that make Ms. Durcal's teaching particularly effective? Which aspect of her teaching would you most like to emulate?

ACTIVITIES

Create a concept map. Write "What I value as a teacher" in the center. Next write your professed values around the center and connect these with lines to this topic. Then create a second concept map with what you think are Ms. Durcal's values.

1. How similar or different are your professed values and Ms. Durcal's?

2. Ms. Durcal commented, "I understand where these children are coming from." Do any of your values resonate with this statement?

3. Do any of your values resonate with Mrs. Durcal's comment that many educators "look through their eyes with bias, prejudice, and a fear of not knowing how to teach these kids to read?"

DISCUSSION QUESTIONS

1. What are Ms. Durcal's strengths as a teacher?

2. What stood out about Ms. Durcal's reading instruction? What does she emphasize?

3. If your own child was a bilingual first-grader, would you want Ms. Durcal to be his or her teacher? Why or why not?

Supplemental Intervention for Struggling Readers (Tier 2)

CHAPTER

4

SUPPORTING STRUGGLING ELL READERS

A SNAPSHOT OF A TEACHERS' MEETING

It's moments after early dismissal time on a Tuesday afternoon. Mr. Gonzalez's students have already left the classroom, and with backpacks and lunch bags in hand they rush out to meet their families at the gate. Back in his classroom, Mr. Gonzalez quickly cleans up his desk, pushes some tables and chairs together, and gathers his students' work samples and progress monitoring booklets waiting for the rest of his colleagues to arrive.

As Mr. Gonzalez organizes his materials, the special education teacher bursts through the door with a large box of bagels and cream cheese in her arms for the teachers to snack on during the meeting. It's Tuesday afternoon and the teachers meet after school every week for grade-level meetings. Today, both the first- and second-grade teachers will be reevaluating their instructional intervention groups' weekly progress monitoring data, determining skill areas in need of work, and brainstorming activities. During the meeting, each teacher shares the instructional levels and needs of their intervention groups. The special education teacher feverishly writes it all on a large piece of butcher paper and posts it on the wall for everyone to see. With so many primary-grade classrooms, teachers have the chance to help one another plan for similar performing instructional groups.

During these meetings, Mr. Gonzalez particularly enjoys the part when he and his colleagues have a chance to share their intervention victories and disasters throughout the week. Ms. Yamura, a first-grade teacher, is relieved to sit for a moment and share with the group her frustrations and "aha" moments of the day. Beginning early intervention instruction as part of the general education reading program is not going to be easy, but these teachers are committed to doing it together.

Ms. Yamura and Mr. Gonzalez are two primary-grade teachers at Highland Park Elementary School, or HP. Ms. Yamura teaches first grade and is still fairly new to Highland Park. Although somewhat of a novice in providing more intense instructional intervention and assessment as part of her regular program, Ms. Yamura brings great skills to the table. She always knows just how to adjust her instruction when she recognizes students struggling with the material. Mr. Gonzalez is a more seasoned second-grade teacher and is seen as a willing collaborator. The principal respects Mr. Gonzalez as a solid reading teacher with a balanced program. Both teachers are known to help their students experience success within a positive classroom environment.

ABOUT HIGHLAND PARK ELEMENTARY SCHOOL

Highland Park School is an elementary school on a year-round calendar and is part of a large urban school district on the West Coast. The school includes students in kindergarten through fifth grade, with an overall enrollment of 789 students, including eight first-grade classrooms and seven second-grade classrooms. The school population reflects the ethnic makeup of the surrounding community, with primarily Hispanic (62 percent) and African American (37 percent) students. A good number of students speak a second language at home (43 percent) and are considered English language learners. Most students at HP qualify for the free and reduced lunch program (94.4 percent). Academically, HP has experienced continuous challenges in meeting expected grade-level competencies in most academic areas. According to previous annual state testing results, more than half of HP's students historically perform below or far below basic grade-level standards in language arts and mathematics.

This elementary school is surrounded by very low-income residents and is situated near a large and widely used street with several dilapidated businesses. Given the influx of local gang violence, poor housing, and lack of employment opportunities, school enrollment has dropped substantially over the last eight years, from 1,049 students in 2000 to 711 students in 2007, a decline of 32 percent. Anecdotally, teachers have observed that once families are able to seek better employment and housing opportunities outside the local community, they are quick to leave. Many reach out to extended-family members to seek the necessary assistance to move out of the neighborhood.

Highland Park is not unique in the challenges it faces as a school within this community. Unfortunately, many schools around the country may fit this same description. What makes HP unique is that in the face of poverty, local violence, a lack of resources, and poor academic performance, HP's teachers refuse to let these circumstances compromise their loyalty and dedication to the school, their students, and the families they serve. Teachers often arrive early, work late in their classrooms after school, or use their lunch hour to meet with colleagues, students, or parents. Given the time they spend supporting struggling students, it is a constant disappointment to see these students continue to fail and eventually lose confidence in themselves and their motivation to learn.

> *Highland Park is not unique in the challenges it faces as a school within this community. Unfortunately, many schools around the country may fit this same description.*

Highland Park's Tier 2 Instruction

Examining School Practices. Two years ago, during the middle of the year, HP welcomed a new school psychologist, Sandra Woods, and a new special education teacher, Roselyn Edwards. One of their first assignments at HP included reviewing teachers' requests for retaining students who were not performing well. That year, the list of students up for possible retention was quite lengthy. Both Sandra and Roselyn had excellent training in Response to Intervention models from their respective university programs and felt uncomfortable with the task they were given. They did not believe in retention as a method of instructional intervention for students experiencing difficulty in the classroom. Sandra and Roselyn, however, did believe that something had to be done to help these and other students avoid this type of wait-to-fail decision-making process.

In order to complete their assignment, Sandra and Roselyn meticulously reviewed students' records, including cumulative folders, discipline and attendance records, and intervention action plans from the school's existing Student

Study Team. They also observed students in the classroom and interviewed parents, classroom teachers, and those who provided additional instructional support. Sandra and Roselyn quickly realized that although these students received multiple types of intervention services, these services were not coordinated and failed to strategically and systematically focus on students' indi-

Teachers and staff didn't necessarily need to work harder to support their struggling students. What this school needed was to learn to "work smarter."

vidual needs. For example, when Sandra tried to obtain samples of students' work from the reading specialist, samples were unavailable. No teacher or program systematically kept track of students' work and progress. Highland Park teachers spent lots of time working with students trying to help them catch up, but nothing seemed to be working. Both Sandra and Roselyn agreed that teachers and staff didn't necessarily need to work harder to support their struggling students. What this school needed was to learn to "work smarter."

When Sandra and Roselyn presented their results to the teachers and administration, there were a lot of mixed feelings. Several teachers voiced their frustrations: "How can we possibly do more?" Teachers felt like they were already putting in extra hours to work with their students, reach out to families, and provide one-on-one support in the classroom. Everyone agreed that their level of dedication to the students and community was high and genuine. As a school, everyone was committed to evaluating Highland Park's existing resources and changing the way they support their struggling learners through a Response to Intervention model.

Adopting a Problem-Solving Model. One first step was to increase the integrity of Highland Park's existing early intervention process, renamed HP's Student Success Team, or SST. The SST adopted a problem-solving model in an effort to more systematically approach early intervention assistance for students and teachers. The model involves a team, to include an administrator, general and special education teachers, a parent, school psychologist, and, whenever possible, other individuals with knowledge of the student. Given HP's large population of English language learners, the SST often includes someone with expertise in working with culturally diverse students and families, second language acquisition, and developing and interpreting achievement and progress monitoring data.

FIGURE 4.1 *Problem-Solving Model*

The problem-solving process requires the team to

1. Define exactly why a student is experiencing difficulty in the classroom

2. Analyze potential problems by identifying the variables that may contribute to a student's difficulties, including classroom instruction

3. Develop and implement a plan to address these issues

4. Evaluate the plan over a series of weeks and modify the plan when necessary (see Figure 4.1)

To meet Highland Park's new goal of building a Response to Intervention approach to academic and behavioral support for struggling learners, the teaching and administrative staff received intense professional development in their first two years. This training addressed general education (Tier 1) and intervention instruction and assessment practices (Tier 2) at HP. The first year focused heavily on helping the primary-grade teachers learn how to teach the basic reading program, infuse evidence-based teaching practices during general instruction, understand cultural, linguistic, and familial factors that may influence student

> ## STOPANDTHINK
>
> Most schools have a form of Student Study Team or Student Success Team process in place. Discuss how the Student Success Team process might function within a Response to Intervention model.

learning, and administer a universal reading screening for all students three times a year. During the second year of implementation, teachers focused on providing Tier 2 intervention and progress monitoring with their most struggling learners.

This chapter highlights two Highland Park teachers, Ms. Yamura and Mr. Gonzalez, and their efforts at providing Tier 2 intervention instruction in reading. Ms. Yamura is a first-grade teacher in her second year at HP school, and Mr. Gonzalez is a second-grade teacher with more experience in the classroom.

Ms. Yamura

Response to Intervention for Beginners: Starting Small. Ms. Yamura is a young teacher at HP. It is her second year teaching first grade and using the school's adopted, state-approved reading curriculum. Ms. Yamura spent the first year adjusting to the reading curriculum and honing her skills in teaching the basic components of reading and administering the benchmark assessments within her existing reading program. Initially, it took some time to understand the benchmark data in the context of students' ongoing classroom work and individual needs and identify how best to use this information to improve her general reading instruction.

By year two, Ms. Yamura and the other first-grade teachers attended ongoing workshops, grade-level meetings, and trainings on developing effective reading practices for English language learners and integrating in-class instructional intervention for students experiencing difficulty with reading. Ms. Yamura is just beginning to get the hang of organizing, planning, and leading intervention groups. This year she has made a commitment to focus on her ongoing progress monitoring and instructional intervention planning and practices to help boost her students' academic performance.

Although Ms. Yamura is an excellent and motivated teacher, she initially felt overwhelmed by the demands of planning and implementing intervention with multiple groups of students. With her basic reading instruction under control, Ms. Yamura initially chose to focus on intervention with three students who needed additional instruction, according to initial benchmark assessments and in-class work. Three students were just enough for Ms. Yamura to wrap her brain around just how to implement intervention instruction and ongoing progress monitoring for the first time. This was her plan for at least the first month until she could get organized and feel on top of her game. Other colleagues felt ready to jump right into organizing multiple groups during intervention instruction. However, Ms. Yamura wanted to ease into things and better understand how these decisions might affect individual students and their progress, particularly her English language learners.

Identifying the Need for Intense Instruction. Everything was set to begin with Ms. Yamura's first instructional group when in came Ana Sánchez. Ana was a slight, wide-eyed girl with long brown hair and a shy, sweet disposition to match. When she walked into the classroom that first week of October, she followed along nicely with whole-group activities, sought out the assistance of peers, asked questions when she did not understand things, and spoke in Spanish with peers to clarify when necessary. Working one-on-one with her, Ms. Yamura could sense Ana's intense curiosity and desire to learn. She talked a great deal about her three brothers and older sister, most of whom were students in the district. Her siblings appeared to play a key role in caring for their little sister. These were only a handful of strengths Ms. Yamura observed that first month while working with Ana.

After spending more time getting to know Ana and her family and reviewing her cumulative folder, Ms. Yamura administered the fall reading screening (see Figure 4.2). Ana could identify 40 percent of the alphabet. Her phonological awareness skills included identifying the beginning sounds in words and distinguishing words that rhymed from those that didn't rhyme. The more difficult tasks of segmenting and blending individual phonemes or sounds (such as /s/ /a/ /t/: *sat*) and using letters to make and read simple three-phoneme words (such as *cat, pet,* and *sit*) were more challenging for Ana.

Ms. Yamura reviewed Ana's cumulative folder, spoke with her previous teacher, and discovered that her attendance last year in kindergarten was extremely inconsistent. During the fall she missed at least one day a week and in the spring she came to school late at least twice a week. After making a home visit to meet Ana's family, Ms. Yamura learned that Ana's mother had been ill and that her grandmother took over as her caregiver. Given that direct reading instruction occurs mostly in the morning in the primary classrooms, Ana's inconsistent attendance made it virtually impossible for her to keep up with the teacher's fast-paced, whole-class instruction. By the end of her

FIGURE 4.2 *Ana's Fall Benchmark Screening Results*

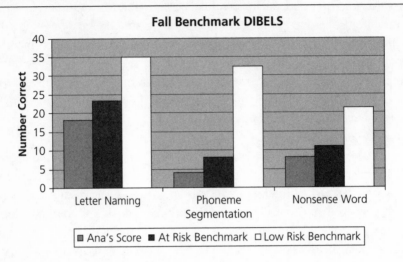

kindergarten year, the teacher had already reviewed the entire alphabet and the class was starting to read simple words, phrases, and passages.

Developing a Support Plan. Beginning almost a month late into Ana's first-grade school year was going to make it difficult for Ms. Yamura to help her catch up with her classmates. Ms. Yamura knew that individualized instruction would be the most appropriate instructional plan for Ana. Well aware of the severity of the situation, Ms. Yamura felt that her in-class intervention support would be necessary but not sufficient to help Ana catch up and make adequate gains. She requested a meeting with the Student Success Team to develop an immediate action plan. The team reviewed Ana's cumulative records, ongoing class work and assessments, and formal and informal teacher and parent observations. Through this discussion the team considered the following:

- Academic and behavioral concerns

- Current performance and strengths

- Areas of need or desired outcomes

- Factors that might influence or affect areas of concern, including instructional and curricular factors, teaching factors, school environment (class and peers), home and community factors, and student-based factors (such as language development; mental, physical, and behavioral health; acculturation factors; and skill deficits)

During this discussion, Ana's mother and oldest sister shared that Ana was a chatterbox at home, speaking Spanish more often with her parents and grandmother, and both English and Spanish with her siblings. Ms. Yamura confirmed this behavior during her recent visit to Ana's home. Ms. Yamura added that she observed Ana using both languages with siblings and during television viewing and other activities. She also observed good models of language and literacy use by all the adults and children in the home, including Ana. The team determined that more time at home with adults last year probably increased her Spanish language skills. After much discussion, the team became less concerned about the possibility that perhaps Ana was experiencing difficulties with language development.

The team tried to piece together important information regarding Ana's experience at school and at home. Ana's mother explained the difficulty they experienced the past year with doctor's visits and how her poor health seemed to affect Ana and her siblings. The principal also added that Ana's kindergarten teacher was new to the district last year and less familiar with the referral process to the Student Success Team. Her instructional style was also known to be more whole-class focused, with less attention to individualizing for specific students. Ultimately, the team hypothesized that perhaps Ana's ongoing absences in kindergarten and the emotional stress she experienced as a result of her mother's illness caused her to be less attentive in the classroom. The lack of attention from the school last year to her emotional and academic needs also may have contributed to her slow progress in reading. In the end, the team identified letter knowledge, phonemic awareness, beginning decoding (such as blending simple two- to three-phoneme words), comprehension, and expressive English language skills as areas in need of support.

The team suggested providing Ana with Tier 2 in-class intervention instruction with Ms. Yamura and Ms. Edwards, the special education teacher. The two teachers decided to collaboratively plan specific lessons for Ana's instruction. The team also suggested working with Ana's family to help them keep her attendance consistent and develop a support plan for homework assistance that would involve Ana's siblings. Exhibit 4.1 shows a sample of the SST's action plan for Ana. The plan addresses school- and home-level factors that may contribute to Ana's success as a learner.

EXHIBIT 4.1   A Sample of the SST's Action Plan for Ana

Present Concerns and Current Performance	Factors Influencing Performance	Target Skills to Address	Proposed Support	When? How Often?	Who is Responsible?	Duration?	Results
1. Primary area of concern is Ana's beginning English reading skills.	*Curricular:* First-grade-level curriculum does not allow Ana to spend time working at her current functioning level.	Learn entire alphabet	Individualized explicit instruction in essential skill areas for twenty to thirty minutes in general education class	Four times a week, during independent work time	Ms. Yamura and special education teacher	Eight weeks	
Currently Ana identifies 40 percent of the alphabet. She identifies the beginning sound in words and rhyming words. She segments initial sounds and reads two-phoneme words sound by sound with very mixed success.	*Teacher:* Ms. Yamura has a good relationship with Ana. Kindergarten teacher focused more on whole-class instruction and did not review basic skills with individual students who struggled with content.	Increase phonemic awareness skills					
	Classroom environment: Ana has a friendly and supportive peer group both inside and outside the classroom. They assist her with her reading when she is unable to complete assignments on her own.	Increase letter-sound correspondence with three and four phonemes, English reading fluency, comprehension, and vocabulary					
She is able to comprehend a great deal in English when read to her, but has a difficult time expressing herself in English. She uses Spanish with peers to clarify meaning.	*Home and community:* Siblings are older, bilingual, and available for academic support at home. Parents are primarily Spanish speakers and are willing to support her at home using mostly Spanish. Mother was very ill last year, and grandmother stepped in as guardian within the home. This affected Ana's attendance and attention in the classroom. Attendance now seems stable. Bilingual home literacy practices are evident, and positive language models are available in both languages.	Increase reading fluency and comprehension	Shared reading at home; preview bilingual text from class	Every weekend, on Sunday	Mr. and Mrs. Sanchez, parents	Eight weeks	
		Increase reading fluency, comprehension, and language in English	Shared reading; preview bilingual text from class in English at home	Every weekend, on Sunday	Carla Sanchez (will rotate responsibility with other siblings)	Eight weeks	
	Student: Ana is motivated and hardworking. With individual attention, she seems to catch on quickly. Initial language screening indicated good Spanish expressive and receptive language, with a relative strength in receptive English language skills. Teacher notices that Ana's expressive language increases with more individualized attention nad interaction. Ana seeks assistance when necessary. Now that Mrs. Sanchez's health is improving, Ana seems more alert during instruction.	Increase success with English literacy–related homework	English homework assistance with siblings	Monday through Thursday, after school	Steven Sanchez (will rotate responsibility with other siblings)	Eight weeks	
	Other:	Increase communication with home	Home and school communication notes	Weekly	Ms. Yamura and mother or sibling	Eight weeks	

STOPANDTHINK

Ms. Yamura recognized the need to provide more intense assistance for Ana right away, from her low reading benchmark scores and poor school attendance record. Her school chose to provide a combination of in-class intervention, home reading, and homework assistance to help Ana catch up. What additional recommendations might you make in this or a similar situation?

Ms. Yamura and the Sanchez family walked away from the meeting with great suggestions to implement in the classroom and at home. These suggestions included using assessment data for instructional decision making, providing individualized in-class intervention instruction, conducting ongoing progress monitoring, providing homework assistance at home, and shared reading with family members.

The team also recommended emphasizing positive, ongoing feedback to encourage Ana's comprehension and language skills. The special education teacher suggested introducing interactive journal writing with Ms. Yamura to help Ana develop writing and reading skills through modeling and meaningful dialogue. The team encouraged her to continue providing a balanced reading program that would give Ana multiple opportunities for meaningful experiences with print and language while providing her with explicit instruction in essential skills areas. We review these suggestions in the following paragraphs.

Using Assessment Data for Instructional Decision Making. Ana's SST action plan calls for intense individualized instruction in essential reading skill areas. Before jumping into planning Ana's intervention, Ms. Yamura and Ms. Edwards looked more carefully at her performance on the benchmark assessments. Specifically in letter naming, Ana inconsistently or erroneously identified the letters *W, V, B, D, P, H, M, Q, G, O, U, E, K, L,* and *Z.* In the phoneme segmentation task, Ana could segment words into one or two sounds including initial sounds and onsets and rimes (such as /r/ /oof/, for *roof,* and /c/ /at/ for *cat*). On the nonsense word fluency task, where Ms. Yamura prompted Ana to read two- to three-letter nonsense or made-up words (such as *wub* or *doj*), Ana sounded out some individual sounds rather than reading them as whole words. She skipped reading letter sounds she did not know or replaced them with letter sounds she felt she already knew. Exhibits 4.2 and 4.3 show samples of her performance

EXHIBIT 4.2 *Phoneme Segmentation*

/r/	/i/ /ch/	/h/	~~/aw/ /k/~~
/p/	/a/ /s/ /t/	/r/	/oo/ /f/
/s/	/ea/	/sh/	~~/ow/ /t/~~

in both phoneme segmentation and nonsense word fluency using the Dynamic Indicators of Basic Early Literacy Skills (DIBELS).

From this information and with the assistance of Ms. Edwards, who is trained in interpreting students' strengths and needs from their responses (such as error analysis), Ms. Yamura developed an initial plan of instruction for Ana's targeted intervention.

Planning for Intervention Instruction. For the first few weeks of this particular instruction, sessions followed a predictable format, combining several activities addressing each of the skill areas in need of instruction. Alphabet review was a must for Ana. Rather than spend weeks of teaching letters individually, Ms. Yamura directly teaches her two new letters per session while infusing several letters Ana already knows using letter or picture cards and kinesthetic activities. Ms. Yamura remembers to introduce first those letter sounds known to have the same pronunciation in Spanish as in English in order to facilitate learning (see Appendix B for resources). This will help keep Ana motivated and moving toward making and reading real two- to three-letter decodable words (such as *map* or *rat*) using letter tiles and template sheets almost immediately (see Figure 4.3).

EXHIBIT 4.3 *Nonsense Word Fluency*

	v		p	b	g
	~~Wub~~	~~Doi~~	i k	~~Vus~~	Nuk
	UI	Zel	f eb		

FIGURE 4.3 *Sample Letter Tile and Template Sheet*

Ana starts by practicing segmenting and blending starting with words having two phonemes or sounds. Ms. Yamura wants to make sure she begins working where Ana is functioning as demonstrated in her benchmark testing while slowly supporting her to segment and blend words with increasingly more sounds. Ms. Yamura gradually builds Ana's sight word recognition skills, along with making and reading words with two and three letters. Table 4.1 is a sample of these activities for a twenty-five minute session.

Ongoing Progress Monitoring and Self Monitoring. On a weekly basis, Ms. Yamura monitors Ana's progress on letter-sound fluency, phoneme segmentation fluency, nonsense word fluency, and oral reading fluency. Ana keeps track of how

TABLE 4.1 ANA'S SAMPLE SESSION

Essential Skills	Time	Activities	Materials
Vocabulary	5 min.	Preview words to be used in activities	Picture flash cards
Phonological awareness	5 min.	Segment and blend two- to three-phoneme words	Color tiles Template sheet
Alphabetic principle	5 min.	Alphabet review Make three phoneme words with short *a*	Alphabet cards Letter tiles Template sheets
Fluency	5 min.	Sight word review: *the, on, is, also, not* Sentence building Model fluency	Flash cards, whiteboard, marker, eraser, sentence strips, fluency passages
Listening comprehension	5 min.	Oral self-questioning strategies for modeled fluency passages	Journal for writing responses through language experience approach

many new words she reads in isolation during her daily word drills. These word drills consist of high-frequency words, sight words, and words learned during direct instruction of specific word patterns. By keeping track of her gains over time, Ana's motivation to read and practice reading soars. Ana's favorite portion of intervention time with Ms. Yamura includes keeping track of her progress. Every week she anxiously waits to see how much improvement she has made so that she can share the results with her mother and siblings. These visible reminders help Ana and her family see how much of a difference this additional instruction has made. Figure 4.4 shows Ana's progress over the year in each skill area, and Figure 4.5 shows one of Ana's daily progress monitoring word charts.

These results show that Ana has made great gains in letter naming and phoneme segmentation, reaching acceptable benchmark scores by the end of the year in both areas. Gains in nonsense word fluency and oral reading were dramatic, but show that Ana should continue working on her beginning decoding skills. Students by the end of first grade are expected to read at least forty words per minute.

Given Ana's intense need in the major components of reading, Ms. Yamura knows that providing her with brief individualized minilessons in these basic skill areas is essential. However, Ms. Yamura also knows that this instruction is not sufficient to support Ana's language and comprehension development in the classroom. To support her more in these areas, Ms. Yamura relies on other strategies throughout the day that tap into Ana's knowledge and experience and encourage her to discuss the text she reads.

FIGURE 4.4 *Ana's Gains During Fall, Winter, and Spring*

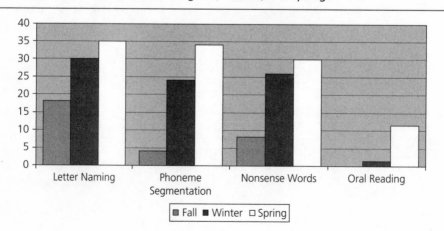

FIGURE 4.5 *Ana's Daily Progress Monitoring Word Chart*

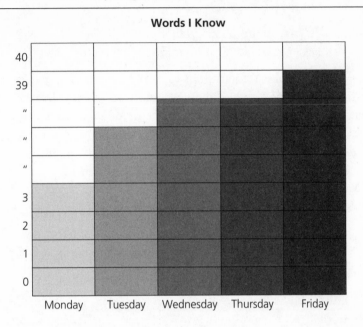

Words I Know

Providing Meaningful Feedback. In order to help Ana make significant gains in her language and comprehension skills, Ms. Yamura gives her meaningful feedback during individualized and small-group reading sessions. Below is a sample dialogue with Ana and Ms. Yamura reading *Uncle Nacho's Hat (El sombrero del tío Nacho),* adapted by Harriet Rohmer.

Ms. Yamura: [reading aloud] "Now, I have a new hat," said Uncle Nacho to himself. "But what am I going to do with this old hat that's not good for anything any more?" "Hat," he said to his old hat. "What am I going to do with you?" "I know I'll put you in my trunk." "Wait a minute. What if the mice get in and start to eat you? No, no, no. I'd better not put you into my trunk."

Ms. Yamura: Ana, do you know what a trunk is?

Ana: Well, it's what is in the back of a car.

Ms. Yamura: Oh, good, a car does have a trunk. But this is a different kind of trunk. This is the kind you can have in a house. It's like a big box where you can store things to keep them safe. Here is a picture of Uncle Nacho's trunk.

Ana: I have a big box at home like that in my house where I keep my old toys.

Ms. Yamura: Tell me more about your trunk at home. How is it like Uncle Nacho's trunk? Can you draw me a picture of it?

In this exchange, Ms. Yamura stops to clarify specific vocabulary. She determines first Ana's interpretation of the vocabulary and then validates and extends her knowledge of the particular word or concept. Ms. Yamura also shows how to use Ana's experiences to help her better understand the story they are reading. This conversation encourages Ana to practice her English language skills, expand on her ideas, and make connections to personal experiences.

Ms. Yamura's action plan for Ana also includes communicating with Ana's family to involve them in the process. The team discussed accessing existing family models of English within the home to help further Ana's English language skills. They also encouraged the family to give Ana opportunities to improve her comprehension of text by previewing material at home in either Spanish or English. For this purpose and for a few other students, Ms. Yamura selects books that reflect her students' experiences, language, and culture and allow for rich conversations both at home and in the classroom. Allowing students to preview text at home in either the primary language or English helps them better comprehend the stories they read in class while furthering their language and literacy skills. What follows is a sample of shared reading at home between Ana and her mother with the book *Fernando's Gift (El regalo de Fernando)* by Douglas Keister.

> *Ms. Yamura selects books that reflect her students' experiences, language, and culture and allow for rich conversations both at home and in the classroom.*

Mother: [reading aloud] *Después de las clases Carmina y yo vamos a pescar. Tenemos un lugar favorito—un pequeño arroyo que desagua en el río grande, el Río Naranja. De camino al arroyo, vemos a unos amigos de la escuela saltando al agua fresca del río. Pescamos por un rato pero no hay truchas. Tendremos que comer otra cosa para la cena.* [After school, Carmina and I go fishing. We have a favorite place—a small stream that flows into the big river, Río Naranjo. On our way to the stream, we see friends from school diving into the cool river waters. We fish for a while, but there are no trout today. We'll have to have something else for supper.]

Mother: *Mira, ¿a qué te recuerda aquí?* [Look, what does this remind you of here?]

Ana: *Están pescando con un palo.* [They are fishing with a pole.]

Mother: *¿Te acuerdas cuando fuimos al río?* [Do you remember when we went to the river?]

Ana: *Se ve igual.* [It looks the same.]

Mother: *¿Te acuerdas lo que hicimos?* [Do you remember what we did?]

Ana: *Fui con papi a pescar en el río.* [I went with daddy to fish in the river.]

After previewing the story with her mother over the weekend in Spanish, Ana is better able to understand the story and discuss it in more depth when asked to review it in English at school. Like Ms. Yamura, Ana's mother also makes connections with her daughter's personal experiences to help her identify with important story elements and better comprehend the story. This makes reading more fun for Ana and a chance for her to reconnect with her mother. During the SST Ana's mother suggested that Ana read these stories again in English with one of her siblings. The team jumped on this idea and encouraged her sister to model the English reading, help Ana expand on her responses in English, clarify vocabulary, and draw relationships to Ana's personal and family experiences.

Once at school, Ms. Yamura taps into these home interactions to help Ana further her understanding of the stories they read. She has Ana draw a picture of the things she discussed with family members. Afterward Ms. Yamura asks Ana to dictate something about her picture. Below is an example of this exchange after drawing a picture related to the story *Fernando's Gift (El regalo de Fernando)*.

Ms. Yamura: Tell me about your picture, Ana.

Ana: It's about when my family went fishing during our *vacaciones,* just like in the story.

Ms. Yamura: Oh, you mean during your family's vacation?

Ana: *Sí, nuestras vacaciones.*

Ms. Yamura: Wow, *vacaciones* I think means *vacation* in English. [She writes both words on a whiteboard.] Both words sound, look, and mean the same thing, don't they? [Ana nods her head.] Ana, can you describe your picture for me? Tell me about your vacation—your *vacaciones.*

Ana: During our vacation my dad teaches me to fish. My family likes to eat the fish we catch from the river. Here I am with my fishing pole, and here is *mi papá*.

Ms. Yamura writes down Ana's ideas. Together they read her narrative while Ana adds more details. Ms. Yamura models this meaning-making process regularly. She also takes every opportunity to draw explicit comparisons between English and Spanish, as she does in this example with the English-Spanish cognates *vacation* and *vacaciones*.

STOPANDTHINK

How can teachers make use of cognates to facilitate the acquisition of English vocabulary for English language learners?

Mr. González

Beginning Response to Intervention: Tapping into Classroom Experience. Mr. González is a second-grade teacher at HP Elementary who started integrating intervention instruction into his daily routine since HP's Response to Intervention trainings began. He spends Mondays through Thursdays working with at least two to three small groups of students per day. Having taught at HP for several years, he was already well versed in teaching the district's reading curriculum. Like the rest of his colleagues, he spent last year learning to administer benchmark reading assessments and using the information to guide his general reading instruction. Benchmark assessments helped him establish which students were struggling in basic decoding and comprehension. He has integrated reading centers and an independent instructional time for students to practice reading alone or in pairs and small groups. He also worked with small groups of students on specific skills and kept track of their weekly progress.

Mr. González wants to maximize the time he spends with students who need more of his attention and assistance.

This term is Mr. González's second year of integrating universal screening,

TEACHER'S VOICE

Implementing a Tier 2 reading intervention for my students who were struggling in reading was initially a challenge. I did not want to sacrifice what I felt was an already rigorous and balanced program where I created meaningful opportunities for my students to engage in a variety of reading and writing activities. New for me this year was initiating benchmark and progress monitoring assessments and intervention instruction in the classroom as part of my reading program. Small-group, skills-based intervention instruction was still new to me, and planning for this instruction was initially daunting, considering my students' varying needs. Before, I was usually more comfortable working with the whole class and less comfortable with individualizing my reading instruction. Forming instructional groups was not too difficult at first. Our school psychologist helped our grade-level team identify and group our students according to our benchmark screenings, language proficiency levels, student work, and classroom observations. The special education teacher then met individually with us to plan lessons, especially for our lower-performing students.

I see the value in doing my own progress monitoring every week, so that I can actually observe how my kids are doing. Allowing my students to self-monitor helped them get involved and motivated them to see their progress over time. The most difficult hurdle at first was understanding how exactly to use my progress monitoring data for instructional purposes, especially for my English language learners. More specifically, I didn't know how to translate this information to actual instructional practices to help improve those basic skills.

After a few meetings, the other first-grade teachers and I started seeing similar issues and requested time from our principal to develop materials (flash cards, sentence strips, and picture vocabulary cards) for our instructional groups. Time for planning I feel was the biggest issue. We depended on her to help develop a schedule for the primary grades that allowed for solid blocks of time where teachers could meet, discuss our students' language and literacy needs, discuss the data and our observations, and develop usable instructional activities for our struggling learners. While we actively planned, our students had instruction in physical education, art, and computer use led by other teachers or had early dismissal.

As a fairly new teacher, I opted to initially spend more time understanding the problem-solving process when working to support my students who struggle with beginning reading. My experience with the Student Success Team this year also helped me change the way I approach my general instruction and think about why students may not respond to my instruction in the way I expect. The special education teacher came into my classroom to model effective intervention practices, like providing ongoing feedback. This year I also focused my efforts on developing instructional units and center activities that would help all of my students work on their language and reading skills in a meaningful and challenging way.

The most difficult component of my teaching involved integrating vocabulary and English language instruction directly and indirectly throughout the day. Our grade level has been working in teacher study groups to further understand our knowledge and practice of vocabulary and English language development for our English learners. There is so much to learn, but I feel we are on the right track in better supporting our students who struggle with reading.

> *My experience with the Student Success Team this year also helped me change the way I approach my general instruction and think about why students may not respond to my instruction in the way I expect.*

independent center activities, small-group intervention, and progress monitoring with his most struggling students. He is now ready to take the next step and focus more of his efforts refining his instructional practices during intervention time. Mr. González wants to maximize the time he spends with students who need more of his attention and assistance.

Identifying Instructional Groups. This year, through his benchmark testing, classroom work, and observations, Mr. González identifies two groups of struggling readers with slightly different learning needs. One group of students experiences difficulty with basic decoding and is generally unable to read grade-level material successfully. These students need more time in some direct or explicit teaching than the general grade-level reading curriculum allows. Another group of students already has basic decoding skills. They can read a second-grade passage without making many errors or self-corrections. This group of students however, reads rather slowly and with no expression whatsoever. This type of reading tends to hold them back from understanding what they read, since so much energy is spent just getting through a page of text. By working with these two groups of students, Mr. González will be able to focus on three specific methods to improve his general intervention instruction: (1) providing explicit, direct instruction in basic skills, (2) modeling "good reader" strategies, (3) encouraging student-centered activities, and (4) tapping into a student's primary language whenever possible.

Providing Explicit and Intense Instruction. With his first group of students, Mr. González identifies one or two sound patterns to focus on per week based on their oral fluency progress monitoring data. After reviewing the goal for the day's lesson and providing direct instruction through modeling, assisted and independent practice, students orally repeat and practice reading and writing words. In small groups, students review word lists and flash cards to increase their word-based reading fluency before practicing these and other skills with

> *It is important for students to practice their decoding skills with text that allows them to experience success with only minor assistance.*

connected text. Using short passages, students practice their decoding skills through repeated reading. The text is written at an instructional reading level where students are able to read successfully at least 95 percent of the text with some assistance. Students who read material at this instructional level tend to read more fluently, repeat some words, encounter few unknown words, and make fewer errors in decoding and comprehension. Mr. González finds that it is important for students to practice their decoding skills with text that allows them to experience success with only minor assistance.

STOPANDTHINK

Teachers will find that many of their students may be unable to read grade-level text successfully. What do you think Mr. González can do to differentiate his instruction and include these students in other activities within the classroom that require reading grade-appropriate material? How can he ensure their participation and comprehension?

Prior to reading the text, Mr. González reviews both explicitly and through informal conversation important vocabulary in the text that students might not be familiar with. Mr. González often has students highlight sound patterns in their passages and draw relationships to other sound patterns and words already learned. Table 4.2 displays what a typical intervention session might look like with this group.

STOPANDTHINK

While Mr. González works with his intervention groups, what might the rest of the class be doing during this time? After working with this group, what self-directed activities can these students engage in while Mr. González works with his second group of students?

Modeling "Good Reader" Strategies. With his second intervention group, Mr. González spends more time modeling fluency by reading grade-level passages and short stories. During repeated reading of short second-grade passages, he reminds students to attend to punctuation that may signal how text should be read and expressed by the reader. For example, in one passage, Mr. González points out the exclamation point and encourages his students to read it with emotion or excitement! When they come to a set of quotation marks he prompts students to change their voices slightly when they read to pretend they are a different character. For these examples, Mr. González "thinks aloud" for students to see his reasoning when presented with specific punctuation. Repeated reading

TABLE 4.2 INCREASING BASIC EARLY READING SKILLS

Essential Skills Addressed	Time	Activities	Materials
[Warm-up]	2 min.	Group: Quick review of words learned (includes sight and high-frequency words) Students practice in pairs while teacher reviews with each student individually	Mini word lists Highlighter
Phonological awareness	2 min.	Teacher: Previews words orally that will be used to teach sound patterns Group: Segment and blend words orally by clapping out individual sounds	Word list
Alphabetic principle	5 min.	Teacher: Direct instruction and modeling of sound pattern *ea* Students: Practice making words with *ea* using letter tiles and template sheets Students: Practice writing words with *ea* on whiteboards Group: Review reading flash cards of *ea* words (folded into future warm-up activity)	Letter tiles Template sheets Word bank (ea) Whiteboards Dry erase markers Socks (erasers) Flash cards
Vocabulary and comprehension (for fluency practice)	4 min.	Teacher: Explicitly teach target vocabulary and discuss concepts from passage	Picture flash cards Whiteboard
Fluency	5 min.	Teacher: Models fluent reading of passage Students: Practice repeated reading of passage Group: Practice repeated reading; students individually practice passage with teacher; teacher records students' errors; students highlight errors in passage	First-grade passages (students' instructional level): several copies Highlighters Pencils or colors
Progress monitoring	4 min.	Students: Read one progress monitoring passage (different for each student) Students: Record progress on personal fluency chart	First-grade progress monitoring passage (one per student) Fluency charts
Comprehension	6 min.	Group: Conduct picture walk of new story, predict what story will be about Teacher: Highlight or discuss vocabulary; identify themes through discussion Students: Fish read (quiet reading) with partner	Whiteboard Dry erase markers Sticky notes Story books Book markers

practice will help these students increase their general fluency and expression and focus more on comprehending what they read.

To further build their comprehension of text, Mr. González models self-questioning strategies by using stories from the grade-level anthology or story books selected by the students themselves. Good readers spend time thinking and talking about what they read and connecting it to their personal experiences. Mr. González has students make predictions, ask open-ended or quality questions, make connections between

> *Good readers spend time thinking and talking about what they read and connecting it to their personal experiences.*

what they read and other stories or personal experiences, visualize passages, and clarify information. These strategies are especially useful for assisting his English language learners to comprehend and develop their vocabulary and language skills. Some example questions include

- What do you think is going to happen to the character tomorrow? (making predictions)

- When was the last time you or someone you know got lost like our character in the story? (making connections)

- What do you think the author is trying to tell us through the story? (clarifying question)

- What did Susana's mom mean in the story when she said "A penny for your thoughts"? What exactly did she mean? (clarifying question)

Mr. González uses every opportunity to help his students comment on each others' ideas and experiences and direct the discussion. Below is an example of a session with this group (see Table 4.3).

Encourage Student-Centered Cooperative Activities. Mr. González uses Reader's Theater to engage students in a creative dramatization of the stories they read. This type of activity allows students to direct their own learning and work cooperatively with peers. Mr. González makes sure to model the reading or provides an audiotaped recording so that students can practice. This week's example comes from the pages of *The True Story of the Three Little Pigs* by

TABLE 4.3 INCREASING GRADE-LEVEL FLUENCY SKILLS

Essential Skills Addressed	Time	Activities	Materials
[Warm-up]	2 min.	Group: Quick review of words learned (includes sight and high-frequency words) Students practice in pairs while the teacher reviews with each student individually	Mini word lists Highlighter
Fluency (passages)	5 min.	Students: Read grade-level passage while teacher or students record or highlight errors; make flash cards of errors for future warm-ups; review flash cards made Teacher: Models fluent reading of passage Groups or pairs: Read passage third time with teacher	Second-grade passages (multiple copies) Highlighters Flash cards Pencils or colors
Vocabulary and compre-hension (for fluency practice)	4 min.	Group: Book walk and informal discussion predicting content and reviewing vocabulary, terms, and concepts Teacher: Explicitly teaches target vocabulary	Picture cards Anthology story Book markers Dry erase markers
Fluency (text)	5 min.	Group: Students alternate reading individually with teacher, or with partner	Anthology story Book markers
Comprehen-sion	5 min.	Group: Practice two questioning strategies during and after reading related to making connections and predictions	Anthology story Class whiteboard to write questions and responses
Progress monitoring	5 min.	Students: Read one progress monitoring passage (different for each student) Students: Record progress on fluency chart	Second-grade progress monitoring passages (one per student) Student fluency progress charts

Jon Scieszka and Lane Smith. Students take turns assuming the role of Narrator, Wolf, and Pig, as in the following excerpt:

Narrator: So the wolf knocked on the door of the brick house. No answer.

Wolf: I called, "Mr. Pig, Mr. Pig, are you in?" And do you know what that rude little pig answered?

Pig: I said, "Get out of here, Wolf. Don't bother me again!"

Wolf: Talk about impolite! He probably had a whole sackful of sugar. And he wouldn't give me even one little cup for my dear sweet old granny's birthday cake. I was just about to go home and maybe make a nice birthday card instead of a cake, when I felt my cold coming on.

Narrator: The wolf huffed, and he snuffed, and he sneezed once again.

Reader's Theater is a great way for Mr. González to encourage his students to develop their English fluency, comprehension, and vocabulary skills.

Once the students read, practice, and perform the dialogue of *The True Story of the Three Pigs,* the class reads the story of the *Three Little Javelinas* by Susan Lowell. This story is about three wild Southwestern pigs and a hungry coyote. Students later compare these circular stories with each other and the traditional version using a Venn diagram to differentiate the characters, setting, and events.

Tapping into the Primary Language Whenever Possible. Mr. González understands that some of the anthology stories, though written within his students' instructional reading level, may be less accessible to his English language learners. The content and vocabulary may not be familiar to them in comparison to his English-only students. This becomes challenging when Mr. González has only a limited time to work with individuals and small groups of students during the day.

To maximize his time during intervention reading groups, Mr. González often selects bilingual stories for fluency practice so that his students' parents can read and discuss them at home in their primary language. This helps prepare his students to better understand the stories they read in a language accessible to them at home before reading the text in English with assistance at school. Parents are often delighted to know they can support their children's reading at home. One parent shared with Mr. González the following experience of reading with her child:

> *¡Qué bien es saber que leer en nuestro idioma es algo que pueda ayudar a nuestros hijos a comprender mejor en inglés! Nos encanta tener la oportunidad de leer estos cuentos juntos y hablar sobre nuestra cultura y experiencias.* [How good it is to know that reading in our language can help our children comprehend better in English. We love having the opportunity to read these stories together and talk about our culture and experiences.]

Some of their favorite titles include the following:

- Alma Flor Ada: *The Lizard and the Sun (La lagartija y el sol)*
- Carmen Lomas Garza: *Family Pictures (Cuadros de familia)*
- Diane Gonzales Bertrand: *Sip, Slurp, Soup, Soup (Caldo, caldo, caldo)*
- Lois Ehlert: *Moon Rope (Un lazo a la luna)*
- Alejandro Cruz Martinez: *The Woman Who Outshone the Sun (La mujer que brillaba aún más que el sol)*
- Blanca Lopez de Mariscal: *The Harvest Birds (Los pájaros de la cosecha)*

TEACHER'S VOICE

Before starting intervention groups in my classroom, I tried to work with every single student and give them one-on-one time. Now I only do this with my more struggling students, which I think is a better use of my time. I'm doing minilessons during intervention at my students' instructional level and sometimes cover material I review during whole-class instruction.

Our small-group instructional conversations have been the most rewarding for me this year. My students love to lead these discussions. I see a lot of growth in their vocabulary, fluency, and understanding of the books we read. They make connections with other stories and concepts and really get to experience the joy and purpose of reading good books.

Since starting intervention instruction, I have not had to refer as many students to the Student Success Team and stopped referring kids for possible retention. I think that's a big *plus.* We used to sit through marathon meetings reviewing cases of students up for retention. Everyone knew that something else had to be done to help these students. Retaining them was only punishing students for not receiving the instruction they desperately needed. Improving our general reading instruction and creating strategic intervention time during the day helped to address these issues head on.

Our small-group instructional conversations have been the most rewarding. [My students] make connections with other stories and concepts and really get to experience the joy and purpose of reading good books.

The fact that the second-grade teachers get to meet every week has been very helpful because we have a chance to talk about what is going on in our classrooms. It's much more useful when you get to actually reflect on what you're doing with your kids. We really never had time to do that before. It's invaluable when you get to dialogue with other teachers who might have more experience in the classroom.

During grade-level meetings we're even able to come up with activities to help us, rather than just talk about what we should be doing with our groups. I've been integrating these activities into my small-group intervention time. Coming up with lesson activities on our own is just too much sometimes. When we're not teaching during the day, we have plenty of work keeping up busy, like units to plan and assessments to grade. When we get to develop activities during grade-level meetings, we get to talk about how these ideas actually worked the following week.

Making these changes in our instruction requires ongoing support from our principal. There is so much that teachers need to do collaboratively and an incredible amount of planning required when working with small groups of students. We would not be able to do it without her support.

PRINCIPAL'S VOICE

The school-site administrator plays a key role in supporting our struggling learners within a Response to Intervention (RTI) model. I have to ensure that teachers have resources for instruction and intervention, time to plan with one another and reflect on teaching practices and their students' progress, and arrange for professional development when we identify more systematic problems through-out the school, at a particular grade level, or in a specific classroom.

As the administrator, I also have to make it into the classroom to observe teachers teaching. I want to make sure that our teachers are implement-ing effective practices in their general instruction. We cannot make judg-ments regarding students'

> *Parents can provide a rich knowledge base for teachers' instruction and make it meaningful and more culturally relevant for students.*

performance or progress without being able to guarantee to par-ents that our general instruction is appropriate for *all* students. This means paying close attention to how we teach our more culturally, linguistically, and ably diverse students who have previously had mixed success with our general Tier 1 instruction.

Having focused this year particularly on Tier 2 intervention, I see that our teachers are a lot more motivated to work with their struggling learners within their classrooms. Before RTI and in-class intervention groups began at Highland, teachers preferred sending these students out of their classrooms for support or even for special education evaluation. Now teachers see their role in their students' success and struggles. They talk a lot more about best practices as a result of their weekly grade-level meetings and Student Success Team meetings. They are trying more activities with their students than ever before. I see higher expectations of students from teachers overall, and as a result of this work students are certainly improving.

Teachers are not focusing just on whole-group instruction anymore. One size no longer fits all children. I see teachers pulling individual students for brief support and working with small groups of homo-geneous and heterogeneous students, depending on the goal of the activity or their instruction. Teachers are grouping students that need specific assistance and working more closely with them.

My hope for the future is to involve parents more in the classroom. Parents can provide a rich knowledge base for teachers' instruction and make it meaningful and certainly more culturally relevant for students. There are also some things parents can do at home that mirrors what we are doing here at school, and vice versa, that would increase our students' success.

CONCLUSION

This chapter described a school in the process of changing to a Response to Inter-vention approach to early intervention, assessment, and instruction. It focused specifically on two teachers at Highland Park Elementary School: Ms. Yamura, a young second-year teacher working in a first-grade classroom, and Mr. González, a more seasoned second-grade teacher. The chapter highlighted several strategies and approaches recommended within early reading, intervention, and general education instruction as effective practices to consider when developing a Tier 2 assessment and intervention program for students in the early grades. These teachers integrated the following techniques into their instruction:

- Conduct benchmark assessment with their whole class throughout the year to determine which students need additional support

- Conduct ongoing progress monitoring with more struggling readers

- Design intervention instruction reflecting students' performance on ongoing assessments, classroom work, linguistic and academic background, and ongoing observations

- Provide time for students to work at their instructional reading level, in addi-tion to providing them instruction in the grade-level reading curriculum

- Provide ongoing feedback to reinforce students' comprehension, vocabu-lary, and language development

- Consult with colleagues to develop activities for instruction

- Consult with individuals with expertise in reading, second-language acquisition, assessment, and working with struggling learners

- Create time to provide direct and explicit instruction in specific skill areas

- Allow students to evaluate their own progress to improve their motivation and their performance

- Analyze students' assessment data to determine their strengths and needs and guide instructional planning

- Consider factors related to students' academic history and cultural, linguistic, and family background when designing instruction

- Tap into students' primary language whenever possible to support classroom instruction

- Encourage families to provide reading support in the home language or English (or both), as appropriate

- Encourage students to work cooperatively

- Engage in genuine dialogue about text, often led by the students themselves

ACTIVITIES

1. Outline and discuss the benefits and challenges to implementing a problem-solving approach as part of the early intervention process.

2. Research and discuss how teachers can review students' benchmark or progress monitoring assessments in order to make instructional decisions. Simulate this process with one or two measures of basic reading (such as phoneme segmentation, nonsense word fluency, or oral reading fluency).

3. Discuss the benefits and challenges of working with multiple intervention groups in the general education classroom. Develop a plan to adequately address these challenges.

4. Organize a debate about the pros and cons of retaining students. Complete this debate with a discussion of retention practices at your site while considering the information learned from the debate.

DISCUSSION QUESTIONS

1. Highland Park recently restructured its early intervention process. Share how your school site implements Student Success Teams. What seems to be working and not working? How might a problem-solving approach work at your site?

2. In the chapter, Ana is a student who experienced a lot of failure during her kindergarten year. Somehow Ana was falling through the cracks. How do you think Highland Park streamlined its referral process? What else can the school do?

3. Ms. Yamura worked hard to provide Ana with sufficient feedback during instruction to help her make gains. What are some examples of purposeful feedback that teachers can use during intervention instruction?

4. Mr. González sent bilingual books home for students who needed more support in comprehending weekly story book readings. How can teachers reinforce the practice of shared reading in the home and encourage limited-English-speaking parents to support beginning reading skills?

Three

Intensive Instruction for Students with Significant Learning Needs (Tier 3)

CHAPTER

5

SPECIAL EDUCATION IN A PULL-OUT SETTING

A SNAPSHOT OF THE CLASSROOM

Manuel and Angie enter Ms. Liana Ascencio's special education resource classroom carrying their homework and pencils in their hands. They are giggling as they scramble through the door, each trying to push ahead to be the first one into the classroom. The commotion of their entry attracts Ms. Ascencio's attention. Without skipping a beat in the small-group lesson that is in progress, she makes eye contact with them, frowns her disapproval at the interruption, and points to the cabinet that contains their folders with the day's work. They clearly know the routine, and they are expected to get down to business. They must get out their folders and begin a paired reading of a passage that they will soon be reading with the teacher during their own group lesson. First, though, they skip to a chart on the wall to check the results of yesterday's timed multiplication facts test. Both children smile broadly as they see their latest scores are higher on the line graph than the previous week's. They give each other a high five before settling into their paired reading.

Ms. Ascencio is known for her down-to-business approach to teaching English language learners (ELLs) who are also students with disabilities. To a casual observer, she seems intensely focused on results. She fills every teachable moment with academic instruction and English language support, seeming to push her students to new heights daily. She sets high expectations for her students both behaviorally and academically. However, her students are well aware that her demanding teaching style means that she cares deeply for them. She is warm, compassionate, and supportive of her students and their families as members of this ELL community.

ABOUT OLIVE STREET ELEMENTARY SCHOOL

This school is situated in an older part of the city that was once an upscale, tree-lined residential neighborhood, but now has become densely populated. Single-family houses still line the streets, and there are also many multifamily apartment buildings and complexes wedged between business areas on busy streets. Though there certainly is some crime and gang activity in the area, it is not prominent. Olive Street Elementary is a large urban school, with over 1,900 students. With 99 percent of the school's population designated as ELLs, the students come mostly from low-income families with one or both parents working multiple jobs to support their extended family. Although there are no official school records of the details of families' backgrounds, the principal estimates that about 60 percent of the ELL students are second-generation Mexican American immigrants, meaning that their parents immigrated and their children were born in the United States. The backgrounds of the other 40 percent vary, with some recent immigrants, some third-generation, and some from other Latin American countries. Spanish is the first language of nearly all the students, though many of the families speak at least some English.

The teaching staff of Olive Street School is diverse. About one-third of the teachers' first language is Spanish, and a handful of them grew up in this same neighborhood. As in many urban schools, there are numerous new and inexperienced teachers and a high turnover rate, but about 30 percent have been at this school over five years, with about ten veteran teachers who have been at the school for many years. The principal, Ms. Avila, has worked hard to establish a collaborative spirit among the teachers and staff, and she is well liked by her staff, the students, and their parents.

This is a large, bustling school campus. The elementary school is one part of the preschool-through-eighth-grade Olive Street School Complex, housing about a thousand students. There is a middle school on the same property and students transition to middle school in sixth grade. The preschool and family center reside in one wing of the school. These programs are supported with Title I and other funding. The family center offers classes to help parents get involved as volunteers in the school, to teach them to speak English, and to support family literacy.

THE SPECIAL EDUCATION PROGRAM AT OLIVE STREET ELEMENTARY

Ms. Ascencio, the special education teacher who is the focus of this chapter, has been at the school for three years. She grew up as an ELL student in a neighboring community after her parents immigrated to the United States prior to her birth. Spanish was her first language. Ms. Ascencio graduated from a nearby high school and went to university in the city. She always wanted to be a teacher and became inspired to teach special education while she was in high school. For one semester, she volunteered in a special education classroom in an urban elementary school. During her college years, she worked part-time as an instructional aide. She loved being around the children and watching them learn new things, despite the difficulties caused by their disabilities. She is certified to teach both general and special education, with an added authorization to teach ELLs.

Ms. Ascencio is part of a strong special education team. She is one of two resource specialists at the elementary site, and they share a classroom and two paraprofessionals. There are two additional special educators in self-contained classes for students with more significant learning and behavioral needs and students with severe disabilities. Additionally, there are three special education teachers at the middle school on campus.

The Resource Specialist Program

The resource specialist program operates as a partial inclusion program. Ms. Ascencio, the other resource teacher, and the two paraprofessionals have a schedule for collaboration in the general education classrooms of their students. They felt it was also important to schedule a pull-out time in their instructional day, because many of the students score more than a year below grade level in reading or mathematics. Most of the students come to the resource room for an hour a day, four days a week, and the special education team goes into the general education classrooms for thirty to sixty minutes a day, depending on the number of students in the class and the subjects taught. Additionally, they have weekly planning meetings with the general education teachers during scheduled grade-level planning time to design accommodations for their students in the general education program.

The classroom is arranged so that both teachers have kidney-shaped tables for group lessons. In Ms. Ascencio's space, the teacher table is in front of a large whiteboard, and nearby is a pocket chart on an easel and several crates of instructional materials. Most of the group lessons occur at this table. For independent or paired student work, there are twelve student desks arranged in two rows. Both resource teachers seat their students at these desks for independent work or peer activities. The teacher work space has two teacher desks, cabinets, two computers, and a shared printer. The classroom is bright and pleasant, well-organized, and free of clutter. There are colorful, language-rich charts and pictures on the walls reflecting prior reading and language arts lessons. Ms. Ascencio frequently refers students to a chart to remind them of a vocabulary or spelling word covered previously, especially when students are writing and they are asking for help with a word. On one wall, there are two charts, one for tracking student scores on a timed multiplication facts test and another for behavior stickers. Several lists of high-frequency sight words are taped to the cupboard doors to be used in timed practice drills. Student materials and supplies are kept on a shelf.

The special education team has weekly planning meetings with general education teachers during scheduled grade-level planning time to design accommodations for their students in general education.

Ms. Ascencio's Reading Instruction

Ms. Ascencio's reading instruction includes two components: inclusion support in the general education classrooms and specific skills instruction in the pull-out resource setting. Reading instruction for her students centers on the general education curriculum because her primary concern is to help her students achieve grade-level standards as quickly as possible. The school uses a research-based reading curriculum that is used districtwide. Ms. Ascencio believes that her students should learn the same content as their peers, but she also recognizes

Ms. Ascencio's reading instruction includes two components: inclusion support in general education classrooms and specific skills instruction in the pull-out resource setting.

that they have gaps in their foundational skills. That is why she and her colleagues maintain a pull-out option for students who are more than a year behind in reading.

Inclusive Reading Instruction *Scheduling.* Ms. Ascencio collaborates with the general education teachers to help her students participate successfully in grade-level instruction. She also goes into the classrooms during reading instruction to work with small groups of students that include her students placed in special education and also any other struggling students who may need extra support. Ms. Matson, a third-grade teacher, has two special education students in her class: Manuel and Angie, described earlier in this chapter. On Tuesday afternoons, Ms. Ascencio meets with the third-grade team for planning. There are two third-grade teachers who include students with disabilities in their classrooms and two who do not currently have special education students. In this meeting, she follows the discussion related to curriculum, assessment, instruction, or management to learn more about the general education classrooms' current activities. She spends about thirty additional minutes with the two third-grade teachers who teach her special education students. During this meeting, they go over the next week's lessons and plan modifications and supports for the students. These supports include modified assignments and tests, behavior monitoring strategies, peer support, and extra assistance on Fridays. They also plan what Ms. Ascencio and her instructional assistant will do when they come in to work with individuals and small groups.

Ms. Ascencio goes into Ms. Matson's classroom on Tuesdays and Thursdays from 9:00 to 10:00AM and into the other third-grade classroom at the same time on Mondays and Wednesdays. She does not go into these classrooms on Fridays, but instead works individually with students, conducts assessments for individualized education plans (IEPs), or goes into classrooms on an as-needed basis. Ms. Ascencio's instructional aide goes to the same third-grade classrooms at the same times, but on the opposite days. In this way, there is special education support in each classroom four days a week. Ms. Ascencio plans the instruction for all four days, planning what she will cover in her instruction as well as what the aide will do as follow-up to the general education curriculum. Ms. Ascencio typically provides explicit instruction about the vocabulary of the third-grade lessons as well as any other difficult concepts. Her instructional aide typically provides review and rereads passages with the students.

Managing whole-class, general education instruction. A typical week in Ms. Matson's reading class would include 90 to 120 minutes a day of reading and language arts instruction. Part of each day is whole-class instruction. This occurs before 9:00AM, when Ms. Ascencio or the aide arrive. If Ms. Matson does not get through the entire whole-class lesson by 9:00AM, she stops and then continues after recess, when the special education support is not there.

During whole-class instruction, the teachers have a system to ensure that Ms. Ascencio's students will be engaged and supported. For instance, both the special education students have peer buddies seated next to them. The teachers and students have met previously to define the role of the peer buddies. They can provide unknown words for reading or spelling, explain unknown vocabulary, translate concepts or ideas into Spanish, remind students to stay on task, and assist with understanding directions. They are also responsible for filling the students in on what they miss when they leave the classroom to go to the resource room.

The peer buddies know that they cannot help to the point of doing assigned work for Manuel and Angie; the students must be able to do the tasks on their own. Manuel and Angie are not the only students who have peer buddies. Two students in the class are new and are at a beginning stage of learning English. Their buddies are more advanced in their English skills, but also know Spanish and can translate important directions or concepts.

Peer buddies can provide unknown words for reading or spelling, explain unknown vocabulary, translate concepts or ideas into Spanish, remind students to stay on task, and assist with understanding directions.

Differentiating Instruction for Diverse Learners. Differentiating instruction is an important aspect of Ms. Matson's whole-class instruction. She is aware of the language and learning needs of Manuel, Angie, and several others in her class. One strategy that Ms. Matson uses is to carefully consider the types of questions she asks when she calls on particular students. She tries to use very clear language and focus on content that they have covered more than once. Sometimes she gives her ELL students the opportunity to think about a question. She tells them the question and says she will come back to them in a few minutes. She often has prepared comprehension questions written on index cards and passes them out to individual students. She reads the question verbally and leaves the card with them so they can reread it. Then she goes on with her lesson for a few minutes, giving the selected students an opportunity to formulate their responses. She then goes around to those with cards and asks them to respond. She will often ask other students to add to a response or give their own opinion. This is part of her routine, and the students think of this as typical instruction, rather than something she does for a particular student. She is aware that Manuel and Angie, with their learning disabilities, may find it difficult to follow multistep directions or complex concepts. She will sometimes repeat things for them using different words or simply check in with them to make sure they understand.

Language Support for English Learners. Many of Ms. Matson's students are ELLs; therefore, she emphasizes vocabulary and the form and process of the English language throughout the lesson. She often points out the structure of a sentence from a reading passage and invites students to practice using the concept. For example, a story about a boy going to his first soccer match described how he packed his bag. One sentence listed the items he needed: "Ron began to pack his new blue duffle bag. He packed his socks, shin guards, knee pads, and cleats." Ms. Matson stopped here and pointed out how to write a list of items, separating each item with a comma. She asked the class to think of a list of items they might pack for an overnight trip and then called on two students to verbalize their lists.

The following is an excerpt of a typical whole-class lesson in Ms. Matson's class. Note how she emphasizes vocabulary and language development in a whole-class format. The class is reading a story about a baseball team that is facing its rival team from a neighboring town. The team's star pitcher has an injury and his stand-in pitcher is very nervous about his first time on the mound.

Ms. Matson: It is time for Josh to go to the pitcher's mound. Someone tell us how he is walking. The story said, "Josh dreaded the moment when he would have to fire the first pitch across the plate. As he approached the mound, he could feel his knees quivering."

Gloria: He is walking kind of slow. He is shaking, I think.

Ms. Matson: Yes, Gloria, I think you understand this very well. What word told you that he was shaking?

Gloria: I don't know, I just imagined how he might feel. But I think this word: *quiv-er-ing.*

Ms. Matson: Very good. [She points to the word written on the whiteboard.] If you are quivering, it means you are shaking, usually because you are very nervous. I'll tell you about a time when I was quivering. On my wedding day, I had to walk down the aisle in a dress with a very long skirt. I was afraid I was going to trip and fall in front of everyone. I was *quivering* as I walked down the aisle.

Now, you think of something that made you very nervous. Boys and girls, I want you to turn to your table partner and take turns making a sentence. I want you to tell your partner about something that happened to you that made you quiver. You might say something like this, "When I was _____, I was so nervous that I was *quivering*." Or "my hands or legs were *quivering* when I _____, because I _____." It really helps to tell the listener why you felt nervous.

STOPANDTHINK

Notice how Ms. Matson helped her students understand the meaning of the word *quiver* and how to use it in the context of a sentence. This extension of the lesson took no more than three to five minutes, but it gave her students an opportunity to read the word in the context of the passage, hear it used in another context in her personal example, and then use it on their own. Each student had an opportunity to engage with the word in a meaningful way. How can you incorporate this strategy into your own lesson?

How Ms. Ascencio Supports Her Students in the General Education Classroom

At 10:00AM, Ms. Matson stops the whole-class lesson and directs students to move into groups. Their desks are arranged in groups already, with four to six to a group, and the students have designated groups that rotate during small-group time. A group may start out with the teacher at one set of desks, then move to another area for independent work. Ms. Matson sets a timer for thirty minutes, which will signal students to switch from a teacher-led group to independent or small-group work. Transitions are swift and smooth because there is no need to move desks. The students take their reading textbook, their workbook, a notebook, and a pencil to their assigned spot. Ms. Matson works with one group, another has a group reading comprehension assignment, a third has independent seatwork assigned, and a fourth will work with Ms. Ascencio, the special education teacher.

As she comes in, special education teacher Ms. Ascencio brings a plastic file box containing her lesson materials, cards and letter tiles to be used in the modified lesson she will conduct, and teaching supplies. She pulls up a teacher's chair to join her group of four students. Manuel and Angie, her assigned special education students, are in the group, along with Jaime and Maria, ELL students who are struggling with grade-level material. Ms. Ascencio spends one hour in this classroom, two days per week. She works intensively with the small group for thirty to forty-five minutes, then provides individual assistance with assigned work.

Ms. Ascencio begins with a review of previous vocabulary words. The words are written on index cards, and the back side has a picture and sample sentence. She randomly selects ten words for review. She asks the group to read the word, an individual to define it, and then two students to independently use the word in a sentence. If needed, she provides clarification or explanation as

> *Ms. Ascencio works intensively with the small group for thirty to forty-five minutes, then provides individual assistance with assigned work.*

she shows them the back of the card. Next Ms. Ascencio asks for a summary of the passage read during the whole-group lesson. Her goal is to check for understanding. She knows her students may have experienced difficulty, and she wants to give them an opportunity to grasp the meaning. She goes through page by page and reviews the story. Then she selects two pages from the story for the group to read chorally.

Ms. Ascencio pulls out a modified list of words from the baseball story that have been the focus of the whole-class lesson. She and Ms. Matson have selected four words from the list of eight that are likely to be useful and generalizable for the students. These are words that the students may hear in everyday conversation or encounter in reading selections. Following is an excerpt from the small-group lesson.

Ms. Ascencio: This word is *concentrate* [writing word on mini-whiteboard]. Say the word with me: *concentrate* [students say the word in unison]. Let's look at it broken down [writes *con-cen-trate*]. To concentrate means to think really hard about something. For example, when I am solving a math problem, I concentrate on the problem so I can get the right answer. I think really hard about math and nothing else. Can someone else think of a time when you might concentrate?

Manuel: When I am doing my spelling test.

Ms. Ascencio:	Yes, Manuel, when you do your spelling test, you concentrate on the words. Can you tell me the whole sentence?
Manuel:	When I . . . [looks puzzled]
Ms. Ascencio:	When I am doing my spelling test, I . . .
Manuel:	Oh, yeah! When I am doing my spelling test, I have to . . . what is it?
Ms. Ascencio:	Concentrate.
Manuel:	I have to concentrate.
Ms. Ascencio:	Yes. Now, Jaime, can you tell us what it means to concentrate?
Jaime:	To think really hard.
Ms. Ascencio:	Yes. Manuel thinks really hard when he does a spelling test. He concentrates. Maria, can you give me an example?
Maria:	When I write in my journal.
Ms. Ascencio:	Now a whole sentence.
Maria:	When I write in my journal, I concentrate.
Ms. Ascencio:	Very good. Angie, can you draw a picture on the back of this card? Now, let's say the word together again: *concentrate* [students repeat the word]. On Wednesday I am going to ask you about this word. Can you remember a part in the story where someone had to concentrate?
Angie:	The boy who had to pitch—he was scared. He might miss or throw it bad.
Ms. Ascencio:	How does the word concentrate work here?
Angie:	He had to concentrate on his throwing—I mean pitching.

Later in the lesson, the word *elated* comes up. After pointing out the silent *E* spelling pattern, the students have little difficulty reading it. However, Ms. Ascencio's explanation does not seem to lead to full understanding. When giving her example of being elated after the birth of her daughter, she first gives a brief explanation in Spanish. Then, she gives the definition again in English, along with an example. The process goes much the same as above, with students taking turns giving examples, sentences, and drawing pictures.

STOPANDTHINK

Special education teacher Ms. Ascencio is providing extra support to ELL students with disabilities and two other students who are struggling. How does her instruction reinforce the general education instruction already provided in the whole group? What steps is she taking to make sure the students can read the word and understand its meaning? How can you incorporate this strategy into your own lessons?

How the Instructional Aide Supports Students in the General Education Classroom Elena Martinez (Ms. Elena to the students) is one of the two instructional aides for special education. She and Ms. Ascencio go into Ms. Matson's class on alternating days. When she goes into this general education classroom for one hour, she works with the small group described above, focusing on reading fluency and writing. She also provides individual assistance with assignments. In the interest of building fluency at the word level, she uses word lists of high-frequency words or sight words and words with familiar decoding patterns. Each student has a practice list, and they read the words in unison three times. This repeated practice seems to make a difference in the students' progress with oral reading fluency.

Ms. Ascencio has provided a set of reading passages at a first-grade level for fluency practice. Each student has a photocopy of the passage and a marker. First, Ms. Elena has the students read in a whisper voice while she times them. They mark their stopping point at the end of one minute and note how many words they read. Then they reread the passage orally in unison. Ms. Elena stops when they hit a difficult word. She often reminds the students that they should not speed-read, but instead should do their best so they can understand the story. She will ask students to retell the story so that she can check for comprehension. Then she times the students again using the same passage. This time, when they mark their stopping point, they notice whether they were able to read farther after repeated reading.

The second activity involves writing in journals. The writing prompts focus on the story from the reading lesson, but the purpose is to foster the students' use of written language and to incorporate vocabulary words. For about fifteen minutes, the students respond to a prompt that asks students to apply concepts or vocabulary from the story to their own lives. The class will be on the lesson with the baseball story for a week, so Ms. Elena has two writing prompts for this week. One prompt asks students to write about a time when they had to work as part of a team to accomplish something. Another prompt asks them to write about a time when they were nervous, like the stand-in pitcher in the story. While students are writing, Ms. Elena helps students verbalize their thoughts, writes words they do not know how to spell on the whiteboard, provides individual assistance, and asks students to read what they have written. In the remaining time, Ms. Elena provides individual assistance to students as they work on assignments from the reading lesson.

Reading Instruction in the Resource Room Ms. Ascencio uses the same reading program as the general education classrooms as the foundation for her lessons, but supplements with various materials to provide extra support for needed skills. She may use materials from a grade or two below the students' actual grade level, even though the students may have used these materials in prior years in their general education classrooms. She tries to pull out the parts of lessons that cover key vocabulary words and decoding skills that fit her students' needs. She also uses support materials that come with the reading program for use in intervention. This particular reading program was adopted by the district and includes a strong phonemic awareness and phonics component as well as the other basic components of a comprehensive reading and language arts curriculum. She likes to use the same instructional routines and cues and prompts as the general education program, so that her students experience consistency from their general and special education teachers. She often uses manipulatives or graphics to reinforce concepts.

Ms. Ascencio is a successful teacher of students with learning disabilities who are also ELLs. Features of her instruction are highlighted in the following section.

Explicit, Direct Instruction. Ms. Ascencio's pull-out reading instruction is best described as intensive and explicit. Her direct instruction is provided in small groups of three to five students in the resource room. Each decoding lesson begins by stating the objective

> *Ms. Ascencio likes to use the same instructional routines and cues and prompts as the general education program, so that her students experience consistency from their general and special education teachers.*

of the lesson and setting clear expectations for what students will learn. She gives clear and concise directions for the task at hand—usually the features of a particular spelling pattern. Ms. Ascencio models the process by decoding at least two examples herself, accompanying it with a verbal explanation. She breaks the task down into manageable steps and gives students opportunities to practice each step. For example, in teaching the spelling pattern of *ow*, she explains that it sometimes says the long *O* sound and sometimes the */ow/* sound. She adds: "It is important for you to notice that that the *O* and *W* are together. You are used to seeing *O* by itself, but now we are looking at it here as *O-W*. She shows the students four words on the white board: *know, tow, how,* and *bow.* She reads all four words herself. She explains that if you do not already know the word as a sight word, you might have to try it both ways. She also explains how the sentence can help you figure out what it means. "The phrase 'I know how to spell my name' would not make sense as 'I *now* how to spell my name.'" When they get to *bow,* she shows the students how it is really two different words spelled the same. "The actor took a bow" and "She had a bow in her hair" are her examples.

The students then have an opportunity to go through the process with more sample words. She expects a high level of response from each student. When she notices that Javier is not reading along with the others, she singles him out. "Javier, you were looking away. I want you to read this one by yourself." Students receive ample practice with the teacher guiding them and giving explicit feedback. The pace is rapid—she wants her students to have as much opportunity to engage in the task as possible.

High Expectations. Ms. Ascencio is relentless in her expectations of students. She communicates a sense of urgency as she teaches them. She does not let students off the hook, even when they are struggling. Instead, that is when she seems to push harder. By making them work through their struggle with decoding, spelling, or vocabulary words, she knows she is communicating the message that she thinks they are capable. All her students are more than a year below grade level in reading, but she pushes hard for them to accomplish grade-level tasks. Her expectations hold true for behavior as well. Her students are well aware that when they are in the resource room it is all business—that is, the business of learning.

Abundant Praise and Encouragement. Ms. Ascencio may seem to be tough on her students by setting such high expectations, but at the same time she gives her students genuine praise and encouragement. She is specific in her praise, always telling students exactly what they did correctly. After a spelling test, she always makes a point of praising students for their correct words. During her small-group lessons, she also gives specific praise when students are able to do the task. Ms. Ascencio also provides much encouragement to her students. She will acknowledge that a task is difficult, but expresses confidence that the student can complete it. For example, while Angie was working on a book report for her general education classroom, she had struggled through the reading of the book and was having difficulty getting her ideas organized. Ms. Ascencio said, "Angie, you were able to tell me about the book. I know you can think of three important events in the story. If you can tell me, then you can write it. Remember that you need to make the book sound interesting, so someone else will want to read it. You can do that if you really think about it."

Behavioral and Social Support. Ms. Ascencio puts much effort into helping her students adjust socially and behaviorally. She attends to the whole child, not just the immediate learning goals. Between and during lessons, she often talks with them about how to be considerate and helpful, how to interact with other students and adults, and how to be part of a group. This occurs in the general education and special education classrooms, on the playground, in the halls, and after school. Whenever she notices an opportunity to point out how a student can be more socially adept, she takes the opportunity. While she was in Ms. Matson's classroom, Ms. Ascencio pulled Angie aside and reminded her that she needed to help her group with the poster they were making. Angie whined a little, and Ms. Ascencio gave her an animated frown and told her that it was her responsibility to do her part. Angie would have to ignore the student who was annoying her and contribute to the poster like everyone else.

High Level of Student Engagement. Ms. Ascencio provides frequent opportunities for her students to actually do a task. They spend more time constructing, writing, reading, or drawing objects than they do listening passively. Her reading lessons often include letter tiles, mini-whiteboards, journal writing, and reading aloud. Even in the small-group setting, she often asks students to read chorally because she does not want some students to sit and wait while one of them reads. Using manipulatives and mini-whiteboards helps with motivation and keeps students actively engaged.

Integration of English Language Instruction. Most of the students in the special education program at Olive Street Elementary are designated as ELLs. Ms. Ascencio knows that learning the English language is a long process that requires constant and intensive focus. During each reading lesson, she fluidly integrates vocabulary, grammar, and language development into the routine. This process involves frequent review and building on students' prior knowledge and experience. She often asks students to give a personal example of a vocabulary word or relate what they are reading to their personal lives. For example, when they read a story about a grandfather taking his grandson to his first baseball game, she asks, "Who has gone someplace very special with your grandmother or grandfather?"

STOPANDTHINK

Following is a description of a one-hour block of reading instruction in Ms. Ascencio's resource room. Ms. Elena has gone home for the day. Notice how each of the features of instruction described earlier is integrated into the instructional routine. How do these instructional practices and routines match with your own? What new ideas did you get from Ms. Ascencio's instruction?

As Manuel and Angie get settled into their paired reading, two other students, Javier and Alex, are already engaged in a paired task, taking turns reading lists of high-frequency words using a timer and recording their times on a chart in their own folders. Manuel and Angie fall into the routine of paired practice activities that begin each day's sixty-minute session in the resource room. In a short time, these four students will begin their own small-group lesson with the teacher while the other students work individually or in pairs.

Ten minutes later, Ms. Ascencio finishes the reading lesson at the kidney-shaped table in the front of the room. She had been conducting a reading lesson with a group of five students for thirty minutes. She offers praise to each student as they check in with her before leaving the reading table. She is careful to give praise to each about their attitudes and performance. Her praise is specific and genuine, yet she does not hesitate to offer advice or admonishment to a student who may need to "shape up." She tells Antonio that she is very pleased that he read with more confidence today. She said, "I know you are a good reader, Antonio. When you read with that big voice, you show us that you really know what you are doing. I was really able to follow your reading." She went on to suggest that he focus on using his word knowledge to sound out unfamiliar words. She said, "You know the long vowel sounds. When we do our words on the board (decoding instruction), you remember the vowels, but when you see the same words in the story, you sometimes forget." For Marcos, Mercy, and

Rodrigo, she notes their effort and positive attitudes. Maria needed a reminder to stay on task while Ms. Ascencio works with the next group. She told her, "Even though I am teaching a lesson, I am going to be watching. I want to see you practice your word lists at least two times and then work hard with your partner. Also, you have three pages in your folder to work on. I want to check with you before you go back to class today. You need more points on your behavior chart this week to move up."

The transition of groups is swift and smooth. Manuel, Angie, Javier, and Alex come to the table with their folders, and Javier appears to have the assigned task of passing out books. Within a couple of minutes, each student has a book, a small whiteboard, a notebook, a marker, and a pencil and is seated around the kidney-shaped table. Ms. Ascencio jumps right into the planned thirty-minute lesson. First she previews the story by walking through each page. She asks students to make predictions about the story, describe the pictures, or define specific words. Briefly, she pulls in students' prior knowledge and experience with some words or events in the story. She often asks students to tell what they know about a word or to tell about a time when they experienced an event that is similar to an event in the story. She then pulls out her own mini-whiteboard, which has several words written on it. "Here are the vocabulary words we are going to focus on today. These are important words, and I want to make sure you really know them before we read the story. Maybe you saw these when you did your paired reading."

Vocabulary development is integrated throughout the lesson. Ms. Ascencio has determined which words might be difficult for the students and also essential for comprehending the story. For each word, she models the reading of it, gives a brief definition, and then asks students about their prior knowledge or experience with the word. She gives examples and asks students to give their own examples. Later they will record the words in their reading journals. Each of these ELL students keeps a journal of words added to their reading vocabulary. In a separate section, they also write words in groups based on similar phonetic elements. This week they are focusing on long vowels. They will add words to that section after their decoding lesson. The group then reads the story through both choral reading and individual turn taking. For about ten minutes, Ms. Ascencio walks the group through a decoding lesson, using her own whiteboard as a model and then having the students write the words on their boards and again in their journals. Following the story reading, she ends the small-group lesson with the same routine of praise and advice for individual students.

TEACHER'S VOICE

Following are excerpts from an interview with Ms. Ascencio regarding her instruction for ELL students.

It's really important to focus on students' needs—to provide all the tools they need to succeed. I work on that very hard. I have collaborated with my students' general education teachers to give those students ways to succeed in the classroom because they are doing inclusion. I want my students to fit in and feel competent. My students have difficulty with writing. I want to improve their skills in writing, reading, and math too. I try to do a lot of hands-on activities and use different techniques to really meet their needs. When I am working with them in the resource room, I work with them in small groups or one-on-one to really focus on their specific needs.

As a teacher in the school, I need to use all the resources I can. I try to involve the parents, but any help they can provide would be extra. I assume responsibility for my students' learning. I think that what my students bring from home has a great impact on their learning, though. The prior knowledge and experiences they bring are really important. The more they get from home, the more prepared they are for the lessons. They have more to connect to. If, for example, you are doing a lesson on the ocean and some have never been to the ocean, you have to do a field trip, show pictures, or use videos to make it more meaningful. You would have to help them make those connections so their learning would be real to them.

One thing that is important is planning. I need to be prepared in order to teach my students, and based on informal assessment I know what they need and I look for lessons that will really focus on their needs. I think that I have to always try to build on what my students know. I always try to start working on their level, but build up quickly so they can move up to the next level.

CONCLUSION

This chapter illustrates a special education teacher's instruction in a large urban school. Ms. Ascencio is very adept at building the language and reading skills of her students with special needs. The following features of Ms. Ascencio's instruction are what sets her apart as an effective teacher of ELLs:

- Setting clear and challenging behavioral and academic goals for her students and giving frequent reminders of the expectations

- Behavioral and social support

- Efficient use of instructional time

- Combination of inclusion and pull-out instruction

- Consistent collaboration with the general education teachers to develop adaptations and accommodations for students who need them

- Seamless integration of language and vocabulary support into reading and language arts instruction

- Effective use of paraprofessionals to support instruction in general and special education classrooms

- Explicit and direct instruction

- Abundant praise and encouragement for students and their families

- Extensive vocabulary review and support

- Use of strategies to engage all students

ACTIVITIES

1. Discuss the features of Ms. Ascencio's instruction in both the general and special education classroom. What features best match with your own, and why? What might you want to add to your instructional routine to meet the needs of your ELL students?

2. With your group, identify a lesson that you will be teaching. Examine the lesson and make a list of vocabulary words that you would want to teach. Remember that Ms. Ascencio tried to select words that would be within reach for her students, words they would likely hear in conversations, and words they would encounter in future reading selections. In your lesson, identify three ways to integrate rich vocabulary instruction to boost your students' language learning.

DISCUSSION QUESTIONS

1. What are Ms. Ascencio's strengths as a teacher of ELL students? As a special education teacher?

2. Ms. Ascencio and Ms. Matson work as a team in an inclusive special education program. What do you notice about the way they plan their instruction? What are the strengths of their inclusion model? What aspects of their model could you incorporate into your own school?

3. Ms. Ascencio sets high expectations for her students. Even though she gives them extensive praise and encouragement, she is generally tough on them to push them to achieve as much as they possibly can. Do you view this as an effective approach? How do you think your students might respond to this? How do you think the parents might respond?

CHAPTER

6

SPECIAL EDUCATION IN AN INCLUSIVE SETTING

A SNAPSHOT OF AN INCLUSIVE TEACHING TEAM

Cami Macinas and her instructional aide, Ms. Martin, meet at the classroom door of Ms. Lopez's fifth-grade class. Ms. Macinas carries a plastic bin full of lesson plans and teaching supplies because they move from classroom to classroom throughout the morning. Six students with special education needs are members of Ms. Lopez's class in a full-inclusion model. Every morning, Ms. Macinas and her assistant work in general education classrooms, providing direct and indirect service focusing on reading, language arts, and mathematics to a caseload of twenty-six special education students served in the inclusion model. All the students on her caseload are considered English language learners (ELLs), and over 75 percent of the school's students are designated as ELLs.

During the afternoon, Ms. Macinas and another teacher run a Learning Center that provides support for students scoring below proficiency in reading and language arts or mathematics. About sixty students attend the Learning Center. Some of them have IEPs that designate them as having disabilities, and they are part of the special education caseload. Others are simply behind in academics or are being monitored for possible referral for special education. The Learning

Center provides small-group instruction in thirty-minute blocks, with students grouped by skill needs.

Ms. Lopez has just finished a sixty-minute whole-group segment of today's reading and language arts lesson for her class of fifth graders. Almost all her students are designated as ELLs, including her six special education students. During this whole-group segment, they have read a passage for a second time using choral reading procedures, stopping periodically to apply comprehension strategies or discuss vocabulary. Ms. Lopez emphasizes vocabulary every day because she has found that her ELL students need continual review and practice to become comfortable using the words they are learning. In this one hour of whole-group instruction, she has also included direct instruction on the grammatical structure of complex sentences and the use of a graphic organizer for cause-and-effect relationships. Afterward, it is time for group instruction, and that is when the special education teacher and her assistant come in.

Now Ms. Lopez directs students to their designated areas of the room by group numbers. Ms. Macinas, Ms. Martin, and Ms. Lopez move to their respective corners of the classroom and begin to set up for their thirty-minute lessons with small groups of four to six students, with desks clustered around a teacher chair. A fourth group pulls out their workbooks and moves to a cluster of desks designated for independent and paired activities. After thirty minutes, students move to a different station. Each group works with a teacher—either Ms. Macinas or Ms. Lopez. Each group also has either independent work or a practice session with Ms. Martin. The instructional plan differentiates students based on their needs.

Cami Macinas, the focus of this chapter, is a special education teacher. She is highly respected by the teachers and administrators at the school for her diligent, collaborative work to set up an inclusive special education program that features an afternoon learning center for all students who experience difficulty. She spearheaded a planning committee that was able to leverage different funding sources to staff the Learning Center

Ms. Macinas is adept both at guiding students through challenging grade-level assignments and modifying their tasks so they can be successful.

with an additional teacher and appropriate curriculum materials. Ms. Macinas is a successful special education teacher because she is flexible and easily adapts her own teaching to each general education teacher's structure and management style. She knows her students and their families quite well. She is adept both at guiding students through challenging grade-level assignments and modifying their tasks so they can be successful. Ms. Macinas holds a special education credential and an added authorization to teach English learners. She began her special education career as a paraprofessional and earned her degree and credential while she worked in special education classrooms. She has been a fully certified teacher for five years, with this being her fourth year at this school. All her teaching experience has been in schools with ELL students.

Cami Macina's journey to the special education classroom has been extraordinary. She grew up in a nearby neighborhood and was an English language learner herself. She became a mother at a very early age, and her children began to attend a school near Manzanita Elementary. The principal at the school began to notice her enthusiasm and warmth with students on campus. He approached her about becoming a paraprofessional and soon she worked part-time at the school while her children attended classes. The principal and the special education teacher in whose class she was assigned became mentors to her. They encouraged her to improve her English language skills, helped her develop teaching and behavior management skills through her paraprofessional work, and soon they convinced her to go to college part-time. Over the course of eight years, she earned a bachelor's degree and then went on for four more years to obtain her special education teaching credential and a masters degree. When she began her job at Manzanita Elementary, she felt that she had finally arrived at her destination.

In this particular classroom, Ms. Macinas has worked extensively with Ms. Lopez to design the week's small-group lessons. Most of the students, including the students with disabilities, will require extra support to grasp the English vocabulary and grammatical concepts of the fifth-grade text. Ms. Macinas's first group of six students includes two students with IEPs. Javier and Eddie are ELL students who also have learning disabilities. She greets all the students by name and is careful not to make Eddie and Javier stand out in any way as she interacts with the group. She seats Eddie next to her so that she can readily provide extra academic and behavioral support. Javier, on the other hand, works well with a partner and will ask for help if needed, so she seats him across the table. She begins with vocabulary review and expects all students to supply definitions, examples from their own experience, or sample sentences for five focus words. Eddie has a tendency to stray off task and distract others, so she gives him the first word to get him engaged from the start. "Eddie, can you tell the group what an aviator is? Remember—you drew us a great picture of this yesterday." She is careful to give him a task that she is sure he can do and offers him praise right from the start. She directs all the students to write this word in their journals, and as they do this she writes it on her mini-whiteboard. She notices that Javier is not writing as quickly as the others, so she asks another question about the word to give him a bit more time.

ABOUT MANZANITA ELEMENTARY SCHOOL

This midsize school is located in a residential neighborhood on the outskirts of a large, sprawling city. This low- to middle-income area includes a culturally and linguistically diverse population. Over 75 percent of the 650 students at the school are designated as ELLs with home languages of Spanish, English, Mandarin Chinese, or Korean. The teachers at the school have a range of experience. There are about twelve new teachers—fifteen with three to five years of experience—and a handful of veteran teachers. The principal, Mr. Angelo, is in his second year in this role. The inclusion program began under the previous principal. Mr. Angelo is an enthusiastic supporter of inclusion and has worked with parents to increase their awareness and involvement in the school.

The ELL students are dispersed across classrooms, rather than clustered into special programs. All instruction is conducted in English with a thirty-minute block set aside daily for English language development (ELD). During this time, students work in mixed-language groups in a project-based approach that fosters conversation and discussion among students. Thus, more proficient English-speaking students serve as language models for less proficient students. Also during this time, teachers may provide instruction related to social and grammatical conventions, using a state-adopted ELD curriculum guide. Teachers have reported that this ELD time is also valuable for the students whose primary language is English, because they further develop their own oral language skills and learn to value the diversity of their community.

Like many of the schools in this large school district with significant numbers of ELL students, Manzanita Elementary houses a parent center that provides support and instruction for parents and fosters parent involvement in the school community. A community preschool is also on site to offer young mothers time to work and learn in the parent center. Teachers find it helpful to have many of the parents on the campus, because it promotes a sense of community and facilitates teacher-parent communication.

Inclusive Special Education Instruction at Manzanita Elementary School

Ms. Macinas is one of three special educators and five paraprofessionals who form the special education team at Manzanita Elementary. One special education teacher and two aides work with students with moderate to severe disabilities and the classrooms that include them. Ms. Macinas and her aide work primarily with the fourth- and fifth-grade classrooms while the other teacher and her aide work with younger students, all in an inclusion model. Most of the students they serve have learning disabilities and are also designated as ELLs. During the afternoon, Ms. Macinas and her lower-grade counterpart run the Learning Center, to be described later in this chapter. Here we follow along with the inclusive reading and language arts lesson in progress in Ms. Lopez's fifth-grade classroom. We will examine how Ms. Macinas works with the classroom teacher to plan and deliver effective instruction that provides support for ELLs with and without disabilities, working at varying skill levels.

Collaborative Lesson Planning. Ms. Macinas works directly with two fourth-grade and two fifth-grade teachers. When the teachers at Manzanita adopted an inclusion model, the teachers decided it would be easier for collaboration if they clustered special education students into fewer classrooms at each grade level, rather than try to collaborate with too many classroom teachers. Because they use the inclusion model, the general education classrooms that include students with disabilities have slightly lower class sizes. Collaborative lesson planning is an essential ingredient of the success of

> *Collaborative lesson planning is an essential ingredient of the success of their model. The school has early dismissal one day per week, with time set aside for teacher planning.*

their model. The school has early dismissal one day per week, with time set aside for teacher planning. Grade-level team meetings are staggered throughout the afternoon during planning time to allow the special education teachers, principal, and other specialists to work with individual teachers for various purposes. It is during this time that Ms. Macinas sits down with each of her coteachers to plan for the next week. The whole school uses a district-adopted reading curriculum, and they have a pacing guide that directs which portion of the curriculum should be covered on a districtwide schedule, and this structure makes it easier for grade-level teams to plan. It also helps the special education teachers collaborate with the classroom teachers. The general education teachers have a similar schedule, format, and lesson design. Ongoing communication occurs through e-mail and on-the-spot conversations to tweak their plans or discuss specific students. This structured planning time is essential, but the teachers always feel it is not enough. Finding sufficient planning time is a constant struggle.

Table 6.1 shows the quick and easy coplanning form that Ms. Lopez and Ms. Macinas use. They are using a district-mandated reading and language arts curriculum and follow the detailed lesson plans in the Teacher's Edition. Therefore, they do not need the details in the coplanning form. The form, then, focuses on how they *differentiate* instruction by enhancing or modifying the lesson. The curriculum follows a scope and sequence for each grade level that comprehensively covers all grade-level skills in phonemic awareness, decoding, word study, fluency, comprehension, vocabulary, grammar, and writing. There is no need to write all this on the coplanning form. Instead, the teachers use the form to adapt the instruction for their students' specific needs. Since most of the students are ELLs, the teachers typically reteach and emphasize key vocabulary words above and beyond the standard lesson plan in the book for all students. They want to reteach and highlight the same vocabulary words across small groups, so they identify these words from the text in their coplanning session. Also, they outline specific skills to preteach or reteach during small-group instruction. These skills might be decoding, grammar, or comprehension skills. Students receive extra practice and support for fluency, comprehension, and writing skills in the independent station and with the instructional aide. The aide can further differentiate instruction for the students with special needs by providing extra practice with these skills.

TABLE 6.1   SMALL-GROUP PLANNING FORM

	Monday	Tuesday	Wednesday	Thursday	Friday
Unit ____ Lessons ____	Lesson ____ TE pages ____	Lesson ____ TE pages ____	Lesson ____ TE pages ____	Lesson ____ TE pages ____	Lesson ____ TE pages ____
Whole-group	Standard: Activities: Vocabulary:	Standard: Activities: Vocabulary:	Standard: Activities: Vocabulary:	Standard: Activities: Vocabulary:	Standard: Activities: Vocabulary:
Small group	Vocab. review Skill focus	Vocab. review Skill focus	Vocab. review Skill focus	Vocab. review Skill focus	Vocab. review Skill focus
Independent	Fluency/ comp. Writing	Fluency/ comp. Writing	Fluency/ comp. Writing	Fluency/ comp. Writing	Fluency/ comp. Writing

[a]*Note:* TE = Teacher's Edition; vocab. = vocabulary; comp. = comprehension.

Selection of vocabulary words is an important part of the coplanning. Their decisions are based on their knowledge of the students' backgrounds and experience. The curriculum they are using specifies in the Teacher's Edition which vocabulary words to directly teach, but the teachers make their own selection of words based on their knowledge of the

They know students need to build useful vocabulary—words they will carry over to other subject areas and life experiences.

students and their language development. Sometimes they select additional words to highlight because they know that students may not really know them and it may affect their comprehension of the passage. They usually cover the vocabulary words specified in the teacher's manual, but sometimes decide not to dwell on a specific word because it occurs in grade-level text with low frequency and they know the students need to build useful vocabulary—words that they will carry over to other subject areas and life experiences.

Co-Teaching. Ms. Lopez and Ms. Macinas use their small-group planning form to make it easier for Ms. Macinas to jump into the grade-level curriculum and direct their group lessons. Ms. Martin provides extra support and feedback for students while other students complete these tasks independently or with partners. There is flexibility in the groups assigned to the independent station or to Ms. Martin, the instructional aide. Both Ms. Lopez and Ms. Macinas follow the same structure and teach the same content, but differentiate their

Both Ms. Lopez and Ms. Macinas follow the same structure and teach the same content, but differentiate their instruction according to the needs of the groups.

instruction according to the needs of the groups. The students with disabilities are dispersed across groups, but they spend less time working in the independent station than other students. When it is their group's time for the independent station, they may slip into Ms. Martin's group or work with a peer buddy. By including the students with disabilities across groups, both teachers have opportunities to work with these students in the small-group setting. At first, they were worried that the students might miss out on the extra support, but with consultation Ms. Lopez developed the ability to provide such support, and working with the special education students in this format helped her to feel a sense of joint responsibility for their learning. Ms. Macinas spends additional time with the students in the Learning Center, so she is confident that they are not missing out on their specialized instruction. Their weekly consultation meetings are rich with discussion about individual students and their successes and challenges.

Table 6.2 shows how the groups rotate to allow each group to spend time with each teacher, the instructional aide for guided practice, and the independent or partner station. The special education students are paired with a more able reader during the independent station time using a buddy system. The assigned partner checks in with their buddy to see if they have questions or need assistance. Sometimes all the students work with partners to do paired reading for fluency practice. Often one or two of the students with disabilities may be pulled into Ms. Martin's group for guided practice rather than go to the independent station if they have difficulty working in the independent format or if they are struggling with a particular skill.

STOPANDTHINK

Consider the factors that go into making coplanning successful. Schedules, curriculum, teachers' styles, and other factors affect how well teachers can collaboratively plan their lessons. Discuss the advantages and disadvantages of coplanning. What steps would you need to take to make coplanning continue to work?

TABLE 6.2   ROTATION OF GROUPS BY GROUP NUMBER

	Ms. Lopez		Ms. Macinas		Ms. Martin		Independent	
	10:00	10:30	10:00	10:30	10:00	10:30	10:00	10:30
Mon	1	3	2	4	3	2	4	1
Tues	2	4	1	3	4	1	3	2
Wed	1	3	2	4	3	2	4	1
Thurs	2	4	1	3	4	1	3	2
Fri	1	3	2	4	3	2	4	1

Differentiating Instruction. How do these teachers differentiate instruction for their ELL students with varying needs? Ms. Macinas, the special education teacher, may focus on fewer vocabulary words, spend additional time on a decoding concept, or adapt the skill sheet for students with special education needs. The special education students are not clustered into one group. Instead, they are dispersed across groups. When asked about this setup, Ms. Macinas said: "We don't want the students to be labeled by their IEPs. We divide them up across groups, but in every group they have support. We [the adults] know who they are and what their needs are. When we plan the week's lessons, we map out how to adapt the lesson for individuals, regardless of their designation."

"When we plan the week's lessons, we map out how to adapt the lesson for individuals, regardless of their designation."

Occasionally, the teachers will switch groups so that Ms. Lopez has an opportunity to work directly with the lower-performing students. Following is an example of how Ms. Macinas provides extra support for ELL students with different needs. Javier and Eddie are ELL students with learning disabilities. Edgar is a new student who fairly recently moved to the United States and is at a beginning level of English proficiency. He understands most instructions and seems to follow along, but does not yet speak out in class. Ms. Macinas wants to help him speak a bit in the small group. She seats him next to Samantha, who is the most advanced reader in the group and has a helpful attitude. Marcella is seated next to Javier. Ms. Macinas is using a graphic organizer to chart the story elements of the passage that they read aloud during the whole-group lesson.

Ms. Macinas: We are going to focus on the characters in the story right now. We are going to put a name in each box for each character in the story. Eddie, can you tell me the name of one person who is in the story?

Eddie: A boy. His name is Michael. He is getting ready for a big race.

Ms. Macinas: Very good. Everyone write Michael in this box. [She points and watches as students write. She notices that Edgar hesitates and watches Samantha next to him. She nods to Samantha, who tells him in Spanish that Michael is the boy in the story.] Now we need to write three words that describe Michael in the box under his name. Who can *describe* him? We need to write words that tell us something important about him. Marcella?

Marcella: Well, he practices every day. He runs a long way.

Ms. Macinas: That's right, Marcella, you told us some important facts about Michael. You told us what he does, and we are looking for words that *describe* Michael. We need describing words, or adjectives. What would you call someone who practices every day like Michael? [Marcella thinks, and Javier raises his hand. Ms. Macinas nods to him.]

Javier: He works hard. He is um . . . um . . .

Ms. Macinas: What would you call someone who works hard to achieve a goal, like Michael? When you work hard to learn your vocabulary words, sometimes I tell you that you are what? "Javier is . . . " There is more than one way to say this.

Javier: You tell me that I am working hard?

Ms. Macinas: Well, yes, I tell you that you are *hard-working*. Hard-working. Michael is hard-working in the story, and you are hard-working, too. [She writes *hard-working* on her sample sheet, and the students follow suit.] Edgar, I think you are hard-working. Do you work hard in school every day? [Edgar nods and smiles shyly.] What is something that you work hard at? Is there something in school that you really try hard to do?

Edgar: Writing.

Ms. Macinas: Yes, I think you are hard-working in your writing. Edgar is a hard-working student. Boys and girls, what else could we say about Michael? We need to describe him. [She looks directly at Eddie, who is showing signs of straying off task.] Eddie?

Eddie: I think he is determined. Yeah, determined.

Ms. Macinas: Very good! Michael is *determined* to win the race. Let's see if we can spell *determined*. Let's clap the syllables to break it down. Let's start with *determine,* and we can always put the ending on it later. *De-ter-mine.* I'll write it on the whiteboard. Who wants to try to spell it for us? Samantha?

STOPANDTHINK

In this example, Ms. Macinas has carefully drawn contributions from each student. Analyze her interaction with each student and how her choice of questions allowed each student to contribute successfully. How did she keep Eddie engaged? How did she validate Marcella's and Javier's incorrect responses and turn them into positive contributions? How did she help Edgar feel comfortable speaking in the group?

Small-Group Vocabulary Instruction. The small-group lesson moves on to vocabulary. They begin by entering five vocabulary words into journals, working as a group to define the words and come up with examples. The class is working on ten vocabulary words, but the teachers have identified five that are critical to the week's lesson and will help the students advance their English vocabulary. She writes the words and definitions on a mini-whiteboard so that the students who need it can copy what she writes. Other students write in their journals without using the whiteboard. After five words, she stops and quizzes the students on the words, asking for definitions, examples, and unique sentences using the words. She provides praise and encouragement, as well as specific feedback.

Ms. Macinas:	*Instant* means happening right away. My example is, "Instant oatmeal cooks very quickly in the microwave." Javier, what is your sentence for *instant?*
Javier:	I ran to the ice cream truck instant.
Ms. Macinas:	Very good example. In your sentence, though, we would need to say *instantly.* I ran to the ice cream truck *instantly* when I heard it come down the street. Can you say that?
Javier:	Yeah. I ran to the ice cream truck instantly.
Ms. Macinas:	Can you say the rest? When?
Javier:	Yeah. I ran to the ice cream truck instantly when I heard it come.
Ms. Macinas:	Very good sentence, Javier! You could have something *instant,* like instant oatmeal; or you could do something *instantly,* like running to the truck right away. Anything else, Javier?

Javier: I cook instant . . . soup?

Ms. Macinas: Yes, I think there is such a thing as instant soup, like Cup of Noodles. Did you ever have that?

Javier: My mom cooks soup from the can in the microwave.

Marcella: Mine too. Is that instant?

Ms. Macinas: Well, a long time ago, we didn't have microwaves, so we had to cook soup and lots of other foods for a longer time on the stove. So, yes, Marcella, microwave cooking is instant. Instant oatmeal is made to cook really, really quickly. That is why it is called instant oatmeal. The same for instant soup. Let's try another sentence.

In this discussion, Ms. Macinas is explaining in detail the meaning and use of a complex word. Note that she first shows how to add -ly to the word to make a different form. This is not the first time she has added in word forms. She frequently shows how to modify words to use in different kinds of sentences. Ms. Macinas also draws more from Javier by asking if he had ever had instant soup.

Learning Center Instruction at Manzanita Elementary School

Ms. Macinas and Ms. Anderson, the upper- and primary-grade special education teachers at Manzanita, run a Learning Center in the afternoons for struggling students. For their students with individualized education plans (IEPs), the Learning Center provides an opportunity for further instruction toward their IEP goals in reading and mathematics. The other struggling students who come to the Learning Center have been identified by schoolwide screening assessments as below proficiency in reading or mathematics. From 12:30 to 2:00, they run reading groups, and from 2:00 to 3:00 they run math groups. In this section, we focus on the reading instruction as an example of how the process works.

The two special education instructional aides are paid from Title I funds to stay in the afternoon and provide assistance in the Learning Center. Students are placed into groups by skill, rather than grade. In addition to working with students one-on-one or in small groups, the assistants conduct weekly progress monitoring assessments, enter results in a database, and print reports for the teachers. Every four weeks in the grade-level planning meetings, the teachers examine the data to consider regrouping students or removing them from the Learning Center. If a classroom teacher believes that a general education student has fallen behind, they bring evidence to this meeting to consider moving a student into the Learning Center. Students who have not made progress after two or three months in the Learning Center are usually moved into the Student Study Team process for monitoring and consideration for special education referral.

The focus of the Learning Center is not necessarily to further develop students' language proficiency. Rather, it is a time to focus on specific foundational skills that are difficult to address in the context of the bustling and busy general classroom. Here the instruction is provided in small groups, with constant monitoring and adjustment to fit the instruction to the students' academic

The Learning Center focuses on specific foundational skills that are difficult to address in the context of the bustling and busy general classroom.

needs. According to Ms. Macinas, the instruction provided in the Learning Center is not specifically adjusted for students who are ELLs. They do not target vocabulary or language proficiency because these are covered primarily in the general education classroom. She does feel, however, that the small-group format and targeted skills instruction help the ELL students become successful in their grade-level classrooms.

Learning Center Curriculum. Reading instruction in the Learning Center focuses on the essential elements of reading: phonological awareness, decoding, fluency, vocabulary, and comprehension. In addition, writing instruction occurs three days per week. The teachers use a respected reading intervention curriculum as their base for phonological awareness and decoding instruction. They supplement with sight word activities and various leveled books for fluency and comprehension. Writing instruction takes the form of writing to prompts in a journal. The prompts typically ask students to write about a story they have read and apply concepts to their personal lives. During writing instruction, the teachers give specific and personalized feedback through conferencing. Math instruction follows a similar format. They use an intervention curriculum as their base and supplement with various materials and manipulatives to focus on specific skills.

Learning Center Schedule. Students are scheduled into the Learning Center for forty-five to sixty minutes. During this time, they spend thirty minutes with a teacher and fifteen to thirty minutes with an instructional aide or at the computer. Each teacher sees three groups of six to eight students for thirty minutes from

12:30 to 2:00. At the same time, each instructional aide works with the remaining students one-on-one or in small groups.

Instructional Pacing. Ms. Macinas and Ms. Anderson use progress monitoring data to direct their planning. The reading intervention curriculum provides a good sequence and simple format for the instruction, but they take their pacing cues from the data. If students are not making adequate progress on weekly checks of basic skills (phonemic awareness, decoding, and sight words), they may spend extra time on those skills by pulling in supplemental materials. The weekly fluency and comprehension check, an indicator of overall reading progress, provides evidence about the appropriateness of the instructional level for each student. If a student makes significant gains, they may move the student to a higher level. If a student's growth is stalled, they may examine the specific skills taught and make adjustments.

Parental Involvement

Manzanita Elementary's principal and staff have made a strong effort to establish a collaborative framework for contact between the school and families. The student population is diverse, with parents of different cultural and linguistic groups. Ms. Macinas is constantly learning about the traditions and perspectives of the different cultural groups represented at the school. She has an easy, approachable manner with parents and is very professional in her interactions. She tries to listen as much as she speaks when meeting with parents.

The principal encourages teachers to contact parents for positive reasons more often than for negative ones. Since some parents use the services at the parent center, that is a natural place for teachers and parents to interact informally. However, the teachers are aware that not all parents use the center facilities. Many of the parents are working during the school day and come by the school only to drop off or pick up their children.

The school has recently instated an e-mail communication service for parents. At the open house held at the beginning of the year, teachers gave out a flyer with their school e-mail address and a direct phone line, explaining that they wanted to be in close touch with families. They explained that they would contact parents to remind them of upcoming events, tell them about student accomplishments, or communicate about a specific problem. In return, parents were told to feel free to contact the teacher by e-mail or telephone. Teachers gave out a simple form for parents to fill out with their e-mail address, cell phone number, and contact information if a relative was providing child care after school. This system has greatly increased the ongoing communication between teachers and parents.

Ms. Macinas reports that being in touch with her students' parents has greatly enhanced her ability to learn about her students' backgrounds and experiences. It has also helped build rapport with her students. Javier's mother is on campus frequently, and his younger sister attends the campus preschool. His mother has been attending English class for parents in the morning and helping out with the preschoolers on the playground. As Ms. Macinas and Javier's mother pass in the halls, they greet each other warmly and can share tidbits of news about Javier's learning. Ms. Macinas has had a bit more difficulty staying in touch with Eddie's family. His mother is a single parent and works two jobs. Eddie comes to school with a neighbor and two nights a week stays with an aunt. However, after Ms. Macinas made an extra effort to establish contact with his mother during a time that fit her work schedule, she feels that Eddie is making better progress.

TEACHER'S VOICE

Following are excerpts from an interview with Ms. Macinas about her instruction for ELL students. She is constantly aware of students' language learning needs while also focusing on teaching to grade-level standards. Additionally, she speaks about the importance of family support.

This year we really tried to incorporate a lot of the academic language of reading, so that when we were teaching the comprehension strategies we gave it a name saying that we were *summarizing* or *paraphrasing* or *predicting.* The students wouldn't know if I told them to paraphrase something they had just read; they wouldn't know what that was unless we specifically addressed that as part of our vocabulary instruction, giving them the academic language of reading. So my instruction has to include that as well. Also, when we're going over just the grammar part of reading, we have to really reinforce the academic language of that too. For example, we say, "This is an action word, and it's called a verb. This is the person who is doing the action. That's the subject." When I started doing this, the classroom teachers I work with began to do it more with the whole class, so what I was doing in small groups really reinforced what they were doing. I try to do this briefly, but I really do it more when I am teaching reading and language arts, maybe even diagramming sentences once in a while. Now that may label me as "old school," but I found that it really helped a lot. It helps to explain to students what is really happening in the language they are hearing all day long in the classroom. In small groups, we can really take it apart and talk about it. I find that it helps them to form sentences—well, that's more of a writing skill—but it's all connected: reading, writing, and oral language.

Our reading program is very structured, so in small groups we go over their reading passages, but any time that I can I veer off and pick a book with a related topic so they get more information about the topic we are reading about. There is so much instruction happening in the small groups. We cover the mechanics and skills, but also really hit vocabulary and comprehension very hard. My students [with disabilities] do so much better in the whole-class time when we reinforce their skills in the small group. I loved the idea of inclusion for social reasons, but I didn't think my students would make so much progress academically! It is great to be able to go into an IEP meeting and tell the parents and everyone how much progress they have made.

One thing that I really think about a lot is the cultural backgrounds of my students. Their cultural values affect the students in seeing themselves as students or as successful or serious about school. They affect their relationship with the teacher too.

One thing that comes up is that the families may not have materials available to them to use at home and so I try to provide opportunities for them. If they don't have reading material at home, I give them books to take home. I encourage them to do that all the time. Also, I often have students come in during lunch or after school so I can read with them. I have peer tutors who read with them because when they go home, both parents may be working and there is no one at home that has the time or they don't feel comfortable reading in English. I encourage them to read in their native language if they can't read in English. I try to talk to the parents about how important it is for the students to read at home, however they can do it. It impacts how the students see themselves in school and how they see themselves as students. I have really enjoyed getting to know the families of my students. When the parents see how much we want their students to succeed, they seem to get more involved.

ACTIVITIES

1. Ms. Macinas spends her morning in the general education setting and is flexible enough to fit into different teachers' classrooms. What qualities does she possess that make her successful? How do you think you would work with different teachers if you were in her situation, and why?

2. Ms. Macinas is very adept at differentiating instruction for individual students in the context of a lesson. With your group, select a lesson that you will be teaching. Examine the lesson and make a note of the adaptations you would need to make for English language learners or students who may struggle with reading skills or vocabulary.

CONCLUSION

This chapter discusses the instruction of a special education teacher in a diverse urban school. Ms. Macinas has played a central role in establishing a school-wide inclusion model that provides in-class and pull-out support for all students who are struggling academically, including those with disabilities. This inclusion model has developed into a schoolwide effort and has improved the collaborative relationships among teachers and parents.

Ms. Macinas provides extensive support for English language development, including academic language, in the context of her reading and language arts instruction. She also sets aside a time during her day to provide intensive, small-group intervention in a Learning Center that operates in the afternoon. This leaves her morning small-group instruction, provided in the inclusive setting of the general education classroom, free to focus on vocabulary, comprehension, and grade-level standards included in the curriculum. The following features of Ms. Macinas's instruction are what sets her apart as an effective teacher of ELLs:

- Collaborative lesson planning and consultation with classroom teachers

- Extensive vocabulary and academic language instruction woven into the lessons of the general education curriculum

- Differentiating instruction for individual learners in a way that allows all students to contribute meaningfully to the lesson

- Positive and encouraging praise and support in small-group settings
- Time for specific skill instruction for struggling students in a Learning Center model, away from the large classroom setting

DISCUSSION QUESTIONS

1. What are Ms. Macinas's strengths as a teacher of ELL students? What are her strengths as a special education teacher?

2. What tools did Ms. Macinas and Ms. Lopez use for coplanning and coteaching? How did these tools help them to maintain their coteaching model? What aspects of their model could you incorporate into your own school?

3. What features are in place at Manzanita Elementary to facilitate communication between families and the school? What steps might your school take to foster such communication? What barriers might you encounter?

CONCLUSION: PUTTING IT ALL TOGETHER

In this book we have stepped into the schools and classrooms of several successful teachers of English language learners (ELLs) in urban and near-urban elementary schools. These chapters highlight instructional models for three tiers of reading instruction: high-quality whole-class instruction in the core curriculum, interventions and extra support for struggling readers, and special education for students with disabilities. Each teacher portrait demonstrates how the educators support the language and literacy learning needs of their ELL students.

These successful teachers come from a range of backgrounds. Some have just started teaching; others are veteran teachers. Most are female; one is a male. Some speak Spanish, the first language of many of their students; others do not. Some are themselves Latino; others are not. Just as Gloria Ladson-Billings (1994) found in her classic study of effective teachers with African American students, *The Dreamkeepers: Successful Teachers of African American Children,* successful teachers of ELLs do not need to be from the same ethnic background as their students. Yet, like the teachers in Ladson-Billings' study, they do need to make connections with their students and families, get to know the communities in which they teach, and learn to be culturally responsive. These efforts require understanding, being sensitive to students' cultures and background experiences, and realizing the centrality of culture in learning.

All our teachers were well prepared to teach English language learners. They had attended teacher education programs in which their coursework included a strong focus on teaching culturally and linguistically diverse students, had gone back to school after earning their initial licensure to finish advanced degrees in teaching ELLs, had participated in extensive professional development through their school or district designed to enhance their ability to teach ELLs, or some combination of these. They felt that this preparation was essential in helping them learn how to meet the needs of their students.

FEATURES OF EFFECTIVE INSTRUCTION FOR ELLs

The teachers we describe in this book have much in common, and their instruction shares many features. Yet they also differ in some ways, just as personalities vary. Regardless of their particular strengths, each one demonstrates a combination of personal attributes, knowledge, and skills that affect their practice. They all are knowledgeable about how to teach reading. And they all are skilled in providing explicit instruction and teaching in ways that are culturally and linguistically responsive to their students' needs and learning levels. In this section we describe elements of their instruction, pulling in examples from throughout this book. We did not observe all the following features in every classroom, but we did see them in most classrooms.

1. *Keep a Positive, Can-Do Attitude.* The teachers we portray like their students and their students' families, and they value teaching in diverse communities. They all have positive, can-do attitudes, generally seeing the glass as half-full rather than half-empty, even when faced with obstacles. Rather than focusing on what students do not know or experiences they may not have had, they focus instead on what students *do* know and what they as teachers can do to help them learn. There is no blame game here (though we did observe this phenomenon sometimes in other teachers in the same schools).

2. *Be Tenacious and Stay Committed.* Our teachers are very focused on making sure students are learning. If one approach does not work, they try another, believing it is their responsibility to figure out what is most effective. Ms. Ascencio conveys this attitude when she says, "I assume responsibility for my students' learning."

3. *Provide a Supportive Learning Environment.* Our teachers make sure their classrooms are welcoming and offer the tools students need to succeed. For example, Ms. Larson and Ms. Durcal make sure their classrooms are colorful

and inviting, with lots of children's work on the walls, a comfy reading corner with lots of books, and a well-stocked writing center.

4. *Be Responsive to Your Students.* These teachers make sure to provide lots of support and encouraging praise. Ms. Ascencio is particularly adept at providing very specific feedback about what students do well. The teachers model this behavior for their students to emulate with one another, creating a climate where students feel comfortable taking risks and practicing their emerging English skills. Ms. Flores emphasizes that they are like a family, where everyone helps one another.

5. *Teach to the Whole Child and Build Relationships.* Our teachers attend to the whole child, putting great effort into helping students adjust emotionally, socially, and behaviorally, as well as succeed academically. Ms. Ascencio emphasizes this approach when talking about her teaching philosophy. The teachers are very aware of the importance of their students' self-esteem and the value of building personal relationships with each and every student. Ms. Larson does this, for example, by using interactive journals through which she is able to carry on written conversations with students. In another example, Ms. Yamura recognizes that her school's lack of attention to her students' emotional and academic needs the previous year "may have contributed to their slow progress in reading." In the current year, she is doing more to focus on meeting the needs of all of her students.

6. *Excel at Classroom Management.* All our teachers are very strong classroom managers. Though their styles vary, one trait they have in common is setting clear expectations, rules, and procedures, so that students understand what they are to do and why. Teachers are "with it," meaning they are aware of what is going on around them—seemingly with eyes in the back of their heads—and do not allow students to become too unruly. Teachers like Ms. Chaney and Ms. Durcal employ a no-nonsense approach, handling misbehaviors quietly and calmly. Others, such as Ms. Flores, rely more on their energy, enthusiasm, and humor to manage behavior.

Teachers recognize the importance of high levels of student engagement. They understand that the best form of classroom management is creative, engaging instruction that captures students' interest and holds their attention. Perhaps Ms. Ascencio exemplifies this best. She makes sure that her students spend more time constructing, writing, reading, or drawing objects than they do listening passively. She includes manipulatives such as letter tiles and mini-whiteboards in her reading lessons. She has students read chorally, rather than individually. Ms. Flores' imaginative lessons also typify this kind of engaging instruction.

All teachers use smooth transitions and are efficient. They do not waste time, instead they make the most of every moment. For example, rather than allowing downtime while students are waiting to leave for home, Ms. Flores plays a quick game of hot potato to reinforce math skills in the last few remaining minutes of class.

7. *Set High Expectations.* Our teachers set clear and challenging behavioral and academic goals for their students and frequently remind students of their high expectations. They clearly convey their confidence in students' abilities to succeed. Ms. Ascencio exemplifies this attitude by communicating a sense of urgency to her students. She is sympathetic when they are not feeling well or are frustrated, but she does not let them off the hook. She realizes that by pushing students through their struggles with decoding, spelling, or vocabulary words, she communicates the message that she thinks they are capable. By trying hard and ultimately succeeding, they are building self-confidence. Other teachers who seem to excel at this are Ms. Durcal and Ms. Larson. Ms. Larson constantly promotes high expectations and confidence in her students by providing encouragement, yet also demands that they complete the tasks she asks of them. She often tells her class that in order to learn they must take risks. One reason these teachers can be so assertive is that they understand what is involved in learning to read and are confident in their own abilities as teachers. In other words, they have high expectations not only of their students, but also of themselves.

In most of the schools we observed, this culture of high expectations is pervasive. For example, at Conrad School the staff had become "tired of its reputation of fostering poor student achievement, supporting minimum standards, and creating an unreceptive environment for families, [so they] began focusing on high expectations, instructional support, and an inclusive atmosphere for families."

8. *Tap into and Build on Students' Prior Knowledge.* Our teachers tap into students' prior knowledge and help them make connections to their own lives. They do not merely pay lip service to this concept; they really want to know what their students have experienced. Not only are they genuinely interested, but they also realize that students' experiences form the foundation on which to build new learning. For example, Ms. Chaney and Ms. Flores look for ways to connect with each child on an individual basis, such as when they used animals to teach Lucas his letters. Ms. Larson emphasizes that she takes advantage of informal opportunities throughout the day that allow students to draw connections with previous learning.

Our teachers also recognize the importance of building students' knowledge before teaching about a topic with which the students might have little familiarity As Ms. Ascencio explains, "If, for example, you are doing a lesson on the ocean and some have never been to the ocean, you have to do a field trip, show pictures, or use videos to make it more meaningful. You would have to help them make those connections so their learning would be real to them."

9. *Provide Explicit, Focused Instruction.* Every one of our teachers provides explicit instruction in letters, sounds, and words. All the teachers prefer to provide this kind of focused instruction in small groups so that they can more readily tailor or differentiate instruction to meet students' needs. They scaffold instruction so that students can feel successful and make progress toward learning target skills, such as when Ms. Flores helps Freddie come up with a word that begins with *E* or Ms. Ascencio teaches students the spelling pattern of *-ow*. Ms. Ascencio excels at this type of direct instruction with her modeling, clear explanations, and guided practice. In her instruction with Ana, Ms. Yamura is careful to introduce those letter sounds known to have the same pronunciation in Spanish as in English to facilitate instruction. When sounds vary, she points this out.

10. *Focus on Vocabulary and Oral Language Development.* All our teachers prioritize helping students develop their vocabularies and oral language skills. Ms. Durcal supports her students' Spanish vocabularies and oral language development as well as their English language development. Each teacher has slightly different ways of doing this. For example, Ms. Flores likes to act out or demonstrate what words mean, such as when she pantomimes dressing like *científicos*. Ms. Larson, Mr. González, and Ms. Yamura all promote active meaningful dialogues with their students, where the students take turns leading discussions. Ms. Macinas makes a point of providing extensive support for English language development, including academic language, in the context of her reading and language arts instruction. Ms. Ascencio also integrates extensive vocabulary review and support into her reading and language arts instruction. Ms. Larson makes sure to point out the relationships among concepts for her students and emphasize their distinctive features. Similarly, Ms. Durcal uses concept maps and semantic webs to reinforce learning. The teachers all check their students' understanding of words while reading; Ms. Yamura does an excellent job of this when she makes sure Ana knows what a trunk is by having her describe it and draw it. These activities also promote students' reading comprehension.

11. *Emphasize Reading Comprehension.* Our teachers also emphasize reading comprehension. Perhaps Ms. Durcal does this best. She provides explicit instruction and modeling in reading comprehension strategies and prompts students to use strategies, such as when she asks them to predict what might happen next. Ms. Chaney and Ms. Larson do this as well. Ms. Durcal and Ms. Ascencio make

a point of asking students a range of comprehension questions about what they read. They pose questions to their students, not just to check their understanding of what they are reading, but also to promote higher-level thinking skills. Ms. Ascencio writes comprehension questions on index cards and passes them out to individual students. She gives them time to formulate their responses before asking them to answer. Mr. González does something similar by modeling self-questioning strategies. He also emphasizes the importance of spending time thinking and talking about what they are reading and connecting what they are learning to their personal experiences.

12. *Make Connections Across the Curriculum.* To varying degrees, all teachers help students make connections across the curriculum. This is easiest for the teachers who use thematic instruction: Ms. Chaney, Ms. Flores, Ms. Durcal, and Ms. Larson. They are able to help their students develop deep knowledge of a topic and apply newly learned vocabulary in a variety of ways, such as when Ms. Chaney makes explicit the connections between storybook reading and science with *Chicka, Chicka, Boom, Boom; Jack and the Beanstalk;* learning the parts of a tree or plant; and growing bean plants. Ms. Larson makes sure that the activities that students complete in the centers in her room reflect the thematic unit they are studying.

13. *Encourage Strategic Use of Students' Native Languages.* Two of the teachers, Ms. Flores and Ms. Durcal, are teaching their students to read in Spanish. Yet even those teachers who are not teaching in a bilingual school make strategic use of students' home language. The one exception to this pattern is Ms. Chaney, because she teaches the English portion of a dual immersion program, with Ms. Flores as her counterpart. One way teachers build on students' native language is by encouraging families who speak Spanish to read to their children in Spanish. Ms. Larson, Mr. González, Ms. Yamura, and Ms. Durcal all do this. Ms. Ascencio assigns bilingual peer buddies to students who can help them in Spanish by translating important directions or concepts. Ms. Yamura has Ana preview stories with her mother over the weekend in Spanish so that she is better able to understand the story and discuss it in English at school. Ms. Yamura also takes every opportunity to draw explicit comparisons between English and Spanish, pointing out cognates when she can, such as *vacations* and *vacaciones.* Mr. González's families were excited to know they could support their children's learning at home. They loved the opportunity to read stories in Spanish and talk about their culture and experiences.

14. *Set up Classroom Learning Centers.* Ms. Chaney, Ms. Flores, Ms. Larson, Mr. González, Ms. Yamura, and Ms. Durcal all use centers effectively. Centers

provide students with opportunities for meaningful practice in reading and writing. Students rotate in and out of centers on a schedule, thus allowing teachers time to meet with small groups. Early in the school year the teachers practiced this routine with their students until they were able to switch centers smoothly and quietly.

In learning centers students engage in various activities that support what they are learning, individually and with peers. Perhaps Ms. Larson does the best job ensuring that center activities are authentic, such as in her friendly-letter-writing center, where students write a letter to a soldier stationed overseas, or her center where students read books and complete book reviews for their classmates to read. Other centers in various classes include fluency practice, high-frequency word review, listening to audiotaped versions of stories, time on computers, independent reading, using letter tiles to spell words, and sentence construction with color-coded parts of speech.

15. *Implement Cooperative, Collaborative Learning.* Our teachers also value cooperative learning and implement this in various ways in their classrooms. Collaborative structures are especially evident in their centers, where students frequently help one another complete tasks. Ms. Larson emphasizes the importance of training students as leaders to facilitate learning experiences. Students do not automatically work well together, but benefit from explicit instruction in how to provide feedback, how to ask for help, and how to be supportive.

Cooperative learning is beneficial for several reasons. One benefit is that students get lots of practice using academic language. Other benefits are using their emerging English skills in a nonthreatening environment and conversing in Spanish with bilingual peers to help facilitate their understanding. Cooperative learning is student-centered. Mr. González frequently involves his students in collaborative activities such as Reader's Theater to engage students in creative dramatizations of the stories they read. During literature circles, Ms. Larson encourages students to ask each other questions or comment on other students' ideas.

16. *Conduct Ongoing Assessments.* One of the most remarkable characteristics of our teachers is that they all seem to have an excellent sense of what their students already know and what they need to learn. They assess students' learning on an ongoing basis, formally and informally. Ms. Larson screens her students three to four times a year to identify those students in need of additional instruction and provides ongoing progress monitoring for the students found to be struggling. Mr. González and Ms. Yamura do an excellent job analyzing students' assessment data to determine students' strengths and needs and guide instructional planning. They conduct benchmark assessments with their whole

class throughout the year to determine which students need additional support, and they conduct ongoing progress monitoring. They also encourage students to evaluate their own progress.

Teachers rely on more than screening and progress monitoring measures. They also pay attention to what students accomplish during reading lessons and what causes confusion. Ms. Chaney keeps track of which letters and sounds her kindergartners already know and which they still need to learn, by writing on a notepad and also keeping track in her head. For example, she knew that Isabel still needed to learn *J.* Because teachers such as Ms. Larson and Ms. Durcal are so in tune with their students, they are quick to pick up on puzzled looks and provide additional instruction when needed.

17. *Develop Instructional Plans.* Teachers are skilled in using assessment data to plan meaningful lessons that match students' learning needs. Ms. Yamura and Mr. González design their interventions to reflect students' performance on ongoing assessments, classroom work, linguistic and academic background, and ongoing observations. They plan together. Ms. Ascencio notes that she tries to build on what her students know so that she can start on their level and "build up quickly" from there. Ms. Macinas and Ms. Ascencio both coplan with their general education coteachers. This process is greatly facilitated by their principals, who make sure their planning time does not occur during lunch hour or before or after school.

18. *Work Well with Colleagues.* Our teachers value collaboration with their peers. They do not consider themselves to be the ultimate experts and seek out assistance from others with particular areas of expertise, such as another teacher, an ELL teacher, a special education teacher, or a reading specialist. Mr. González and Ms. Yamura consult frequently with colleagues to develop activities for instruction. This appears to be a strength of their school. Ms. Macinas and Ms. Ascencio collaborate a great deal as special education teachers, engaging in collaborative lesson planning, as noted earlier, and also collaborative consultation with classroom teachers to develop adaptations and accommodations for students. Ms. Flores and Ms. Chaney collaborate every day as part of their school's dual immersion program. In addition to regular meetings, they frequently check in with one another about particular students or to share an anecdote from the day.

19. *Develop Partnerships with Parents and the Community.* Every one of our teachers emphasizes the importance of getting to know and working with parents and other family members. They all recognize how valuable this is for their students. Ms. Durcal visits her students' homes and invites parents into her

classroom. By encouraging parents to read to their children in Spanish, teachers are conveying that parents' expertise is valued. Ms. Larson and Ms. Macina's schools house a parent center that provides support and instruction for parents and fosters parent involvement in the school community.

RESPONSE TO INTERVENTION AND ENGLISH LANGUAGE LEARNERS

In this book we have presented vivid portraits of effective teachers at each tier of the Response to Intervention model. These portraits are not meant to provide readers with detailed instructions and how-to steps for building an RTI model specifically for English language learners. However, these portraits should provide readers with a general understanding of what to plan, how to teach, and what to look out for when considering the specific needs of ELLs within this assessment and intervention framework. We provide you with some guiding questions to further your thinking as you continue planning for, implementing, and improving RTI for English language learners at both the school and classroom level. We offer a useful rule of thumb to consider when determining which ELLs should receive supplemental interventions: if Tier 1 instruction is appropriate for the ELLs in a class, then most ELLs will be making at least adequate progress. If most ELLs are struggling, then the focus should be on improving classroom instruction to meet their needs (Klingner, Méndez Barletta, & Hoover, 2008).

RTI for ELLs must be applied in a comprehensive, schoolwide approach that coordinates curriculum and assessment considerations, addresses teachers' professional development needs, and attends to school climate issues (Adelman & Taylor, n.d.). RTI is part a comprehensive system of classroom and schoolwide learning supports. Effective implementation of RTI for ELLs requires strong leadership; collaboration among special educators, general educators, ELL and reading specialists, and families; and a well-established, efficient infrastructure (Burdette, 2007).

Tier 1

1. Have I had sufficient preparation in teaching culturally and linguistically diverse students?

2. Are all students receiving scientifically based reading instruction that has been shown to be effective with similar students in similar contexts?

3. Are students' primary and second languages and cultures considered in assessment and instructional planning and decision making?

4. Does instruction take into account students' cultural, linguistic, socioeconomic, and experiential backgrounds, including English and native language proficiency levels?

5. Does the school compare students' progress and performance to that of true peers, with whom educational background, culture, and language are comparable?

6. Are parents involved in instruction, planning, and decision making?

7. Is instruction differentiated to meet all students' needs?

8. Do I value and build on the strengths of my students and their families?

9. Am I knowledgeable about and skilled in accounting for differences in learning to read in students' first and second languages and those aspects of reading in English that can be confusing?

10. Do I teach in students' first language or use the first language in strategic ways?

Tier 2

1. Do Tier 2 providers have sufficient preparation or expertise in serving culturally and linguistically diverse students?

2. Does the system for progress monitoring include multiple kinds of measures—both quantitative and qualitative—that assess what students can do, as well as their learning needs?

3. Are experts on students' linguistic and cultural backgrounds involved in interpreting assessment data and planning instruction?

4. Is a plan in place for using assessment data to group and regroup students (in small same-ability groups and one-on-one tutoring), to plan targeted instruction, and to make adaptations?

5. Are criteria for entry into and exit from Tier 2 implemented and reassessed as needed, with the help of experts who are knowledgeable about the cultural and linguistic backgrounds and needs of the students involved?

6. Do interventions consider students' cultural, linguistic, socioeconomic, and experiential backgrounds?

7. Does the level of a student's progress match or fall behind the progress of comparable peers?

8. Are interventions scientifically based, and have they been validated with similar students in similar contexts and individualized to meet students' needs?

9. Are interventions provided in the most natural environment possible to minimize disruption and distractions?

10. Do students have sufficient opportunities for feedback and response during instruction?

Tier 3

1. Have ongoing assessment data been collected documenting students' performance?

2. How does each student perform in comparison to similar peers according to level and rate of performance?

3. Have all factors been considered to account for a student's performance or lack of performance, including school-level, instructional, teacher, peer, classroom, home, and student-level factors?

4. Is the primary language considered in instructional planning and assessment data?

5. How do service providers (special education and general education teachers and English language development specialists) collaborate at this level to ensure access to general education content, support with English language acquisition, native language instruction (when possible), and special education support?

OVERALL RECOMMENDATIONS

Effective Classroom Practices

- Provide a positive, supportive learning environment

- Build strong relationships with students and their families

- Maintain high expectations for what students can learn and do, and convey this to them in multiple ways through encouragement, constructive feedback, and support

- Provide a rigorous, challenging curriculum

- Design activities that allow students to work collaboratively with peers

- Develop center activities that are meaningful and authentic and reinforce learning

- Provide opportunities for students to work as leaders in the classroom to facilitate learning experiences

- Encourage families to provide in-class and at-home support whenever possible

- Look for ways to connect with and build on students' home cultures

- Encourage primary- and second-language models outside the classroom to support learning

- Make strategic use of students' native language

- Promote active, meaningful dialogue using authentic text and encourage to students lead discussions that improve their reading comprehension as well as their overall English language skills

- Conduct universal screening and ongoing progress monitoring as well as informal assessments to inform instruction

- Provide explicit and direct instruction of necessary reading skills in small groups

- Help students access their prior knowledge and build new knowledge

- Help students make connections among concepts and to their own lives

- Emphasize the distinctive features of concepts

- Teach reading comprehension strategies and provide cues and prompts to use strategies and skills

- Provide formal and informal instruction in English vocabulary and language use

- Use visuals to reinforce new concepts and vocabulary

- Emphasize oral language development

- Provide opportunities for students to use higher-level thinking skills

- Provide frequent opportunities for meaningful practice

Struggling Readers

- Conduct benchmark assessments, progress monitoring, and other assessments to guide instruction

- Design intervention instruction reflecting students' performance on ongoing assessments, classroom work, linguistic and academic background, and ongoing observations

- Provide time for students to work at their own individual instruction reading levels in addition to instructing them in meaningful grade-level text

- Provide ongoing feedback to reinforce students' comprehension, vocabulary, and language development

- Collaborate with colleagues to support the instruction of struggling readers

- Provide direct and explicit instruction in specific skill areas when appropriate

- Allow students to evaluate their own progress, which in turn increases their motivation and improves their performance

- Analyze students' assessment data to determine their strengths and needs and guide instructional planning

- Consider factors related to students' academic history, culture, language, and family background when interpreting assessment data and designing instruction

- Tap into students' native language and culture whenever possible to support classroom instruction

- Encourage families to contribute to classroom instruction both at school and at home

- Encourage students to work cooperatively

- Engage in genuine dialogue about meaningful text

- Provide sufficient opportunities for students to actively participate in their own learning

IN CLOSING

It is remarkable how closely the list of recommendations we have generated from our observations of successful teachers' classrooms matches the recommendations of experts in the field who have identified effective practices for ELLs, particularly struggling readers (August & Hakuta, 1997; August & Shanahan, 2007; Gersten & Baker, 2000; Gersten & Jiménez, 1998; Graves, Gersten, & Haager, 2004; Ortiz, 2001). These researchers emphasize the importance of focusing on oral language development, foregrounding cultural variables, providing explicit instruction, and helping students' access and build background knowledge. It is our sincere hope that reading the portraits of these successful teachers and reflecting about their practices will help you become the successful teacher you want to be and ensure positive outcomes for the English language learners you teach.

APPENDIX

SUGGESTED WEB RESOURCES

AIMSweb Progress Monitoring

www.aimsweb.com

AIMSweb is an online progress monitoring system for reading, spelling, writing, and mathematics. Results can be reported to students, parents, and teachers using their web-based management and reporting system. Graduate students can obtain access to AIMSweb benchmark and progress monitoring probes after purchasing a University Student Package. The web site also includes instructional manuals and helpful PowerPoint presentations for training purposes.

All America Reads

www.allamericareads.org

The All America Reads web site contains resources and information on reading and reading comprehension. The Lesson Plans section provides suggestions for before, during, and after reading strategies, as well as vocabulary acquisition strategies. The ongoing program is designed to encourage reading and discussion of novels with broad appeal and accessible themes.

American Federation of Teachers, English Language Learners
www.aft.org/topics/ells/index.htm
The American Federation of Teachers provides resources for teachers, institutions of higher education, paraprofessionals, and school-related personnel. Site resources specific to English language learners include helpful PDF documents on research-based practices, guidelines, testing requirements, and educational issue briefs related to ELLs.

American Library Association
www.ala.org
The American Library Association web site provides recommendations for books for children, including many suggestions for reluctant and struggling readers. The online store offers create-your-own READ poster CDs, character and author posters, bookmarks, T-shirts, bags, and other items.

Barahona Center
www.csusm.edu/csb
This web site has lists of recommended children's books in English and Spanish, including recommended books in English about Latinos. They also offer a Reading Partners Program designed to support professional development.

Center for Improvement of Early Reading Achievement
www.ciera.org
The Center for Improvement of Early Reading Achievement provides resources for teaching early reading. The link to the CIERA archive contains key publications in early literacy for teachers and researchers. Some focus on English language learners.

Center for Applied Linguistics
www.cal.org
This site provides lots of information and many resources for teaching English language learners. Topic areas include ESL literacy, bilingual education, dialects and Ebonics, immigrant education, language testing, literacy (pre-K–12), refugee concerns, and two-way immersion.

Center for Applied Special Technology (CAST)
www.cast.org

CAST is a nonprofit research organization working to expand learning opportunities for all individuals, primarily those with disabilities, through Universal Design for Learning (UDL). The site provides users with information on research, publications, professional development, and products reflecting UDL standards. Their universally designed literacy series for beginning readers and writers, WiggleWorks!, is now available in Spanish.

Center for Research on the Educational Achievement and Teaching English Language Learners (CREATE)
www.cal.org/create/index.html
CREATE's research addresses the challenge of improving educational outcomes of English language learners through empirical research. Current research focuses on enhancing instruction for readers in fourth through eighth grades. The web site allows users to subscribe to CREATE updates, e-mail announcements, and a newsletter.

Center on Instruction
www.centeroninstruction.org
The Center on Instruction is one of five content centers serving as resources for the sixteen regional U.S. Department of Education Comprehensive Centers. This site provides several resources for reading, special education, and English language learners. Resources include information sheets, position papers, and PowerPoint presentations.

¡Colorín Colorado!
www.colorincolorado.org
Specifically designed for teachers and parents of ELLs, ¡Colorín, Colorado! houses extremely helpful resources, activities, and advice for educators and Spanish-speaking families of English language learners. The site includes research reports, guides, tool kits, and a learning store. Free webcasts cover such topics as assessment and instruction of ELLs, ELLs with learning disabilities, and improving children's academic language.

Council for Exceptional Children (CEC), Response to Intervention
www.cec.sped.org
This CEC site includes links to several useful reports, position papers, and how-to guides on Response to Intervention (RTI), including some on ELLs.

Council for Exceptional Children (CEC), Division for Learning Disabilities
www.teachingld.org
This site includes lots of information on teaching students with learning disabilities, including position papers, teaching how-to guides, lesson plans, resources, and PowerPoint presentations.

Dynamic Indicators of Basic Early Literacy Skills (DIBELS)
https://dibels.uoregon.edu
The DIBELS measures are specifically designed to assess the acquisition of early literacy skills from kindergarten through sixth grade. Measures are short (one-minute) fluency tasks to monitor students' progress in early reading. Teachers can access for free the administration manuals and benchmark and progress monitoring probes. For a fee, schools can access the DIBELS data system and generate reports at the student, class, school, and district levels.

Evaluating Children's Books for Bias
www.intime.uni.edu/multiculture/curriculum/children.htm
This web site is part of IN TIME: Integrating New Technologies into the Methods of Education. It provides a useful list of ways to evaluate children's literature for subtle forms of bias and to determine its appropriateness.

Florida Center for Reading Research
www.fcrr.org
This web site offers lots of resources for teaching struggling readers as part of an RTI model, as well as professional development supports, links to other sites, webcasts, and recommended readings.

Inside Teaching
http://gallery.carnegiefoundation.org/insideteaching
Funded by the Carnegie Foundation, this site provides collections of multimedia records of teaching practice as well as diverse perspectives on a multitude of educational issues. The site is meant to be a living archive that relies on the contributions of visitors.

International Dyslexia Association
www.interdys.org
This site for the International Dyslexia Association provides resources for teaching individuals with reading disabilities.

International Reading Association

www.reading.org

This comprehensive web site has lots of resources for teachers about teaching reading. Specific sections provide information on ELLs and culturally and linguistically diverse students. The site provides a host of resources on teaching reading, books, articles, position statements, links to online resources, lesson plans, book lists, and resources for parents.

IRIS Center

http://iris.peabody.vanderbilt.edu

The IRIS Center at Vanderbilt University provides lots of resources, including professional development modules, case studies, sample activities, info briefs, and podcasts. Topics include differentiated instruction, diversity, Response to Intervention, and reading, literacy, and language arts.

Knowledge Loom

http://knowledgeloom.org/index.jsp

This site is an excellent source for information on culturally responsive teaching and literacy instruction in grades K–3. Reports include "Meeting the Literacy Needs of English Language Learners (ELLs)" and "Technology and Teaching Children to Read."

LD Online

www.ldonline.org

LD Online is an educational service of public television station WETA in Washington, D.C., in association with the National Joint Committee on Learning Disabilities. The web site provides information and resources for teachers, parents, and students about reading and other disabilities, teaching, and research.

LD Resources

www.ldresources.com

This web site provides a large number of entries on all aspects of learning disabilities and learning to read and provides a forum for comments and feedback on these topics.

Literacy Connections

http://literacyconnections.com

This web site provides a variety of resources related to teaching and tutoring reading, such as word study, sight word learning, language experience, reading aloud, and Reader's Theater activities. Additional resources include organizations that support literacy and information for parents. Their Literacy Connections Store links users directly to some very helpful references, puppets, games, and other materials for purchase.

Literacy Web
www.literacy.uconn.edu/index.htm
The University of Connecticut Literacy Web provides a wealth of resources on different aspects of reading instruction, including multicultural literacy, early literacy, comprehension instruction, vocabulary instruction, strategies, and activities, such as resources for teaching English Language learners.

National Association for Bilingual Education (NABE)
www.nabe.org
This site includes links to NABE's publications, which are available for free online: the *NABE News Magazine, Bilingual Research Journal,* and the *NABE Journal of Research and Practice.*

National Association for Multicultural Education (NAME)
www.nameorg.org
This site offers position papers, press releases, publications, FAQs, and other resources related to educating culturally and linguistically diverse students. It also provides access to NAME's journal, *Multicultural Perspectives.*

National Association of State Directors of Special Education (NASDSE)
www.nasdse.org
NASDSE provides an excellent how-to guide on RTI called *Response to Intervention: Policy Considerations and Implementation,* and their web site includes information on ordering this book. They also offer information from two satellite conferences on RTI, as well as several short papers and PowerPoint presentations that can be downloaded for free.

National Center for Culturally Responsive Educational Systems
www.nccrest.org
This site provides access to an extensive online library, practitioner briefs, professional development materials, self-assessment guides, and position statements.

All are designed to help educators enhance educational opportunities for culturally and linguistically diverse students.

National Center for Learning Disabilities
www.ncld.org
The National Center for Learning Disabilities site provides information and resources related to learning disabilities, including reading disabilities. The LD InfoZone link provides syntheses of research in various areas of reading.

National Center on Response to Intervention
www.rti4success.org
Supported by IDEAS that Work, U.S. Office of Special Education Programs, this web site offers many resources on RTI. Library resource topics cover a range of topics on RTI, including cultural and linguistic diversity. Webinar recordings and accompanying PowerPoint and MS Word materials are available in such topics as RTI and English language learners, and universal screening. The web site offers archived newsletters, discussion forums, and an updated calendar of events related to RTI training.

National Central Regional Educational Laboratory, Multicultural Children's Literature
www.ncrel.org/sdrs/areas/issues/educatrs/presrvce/pe3lk28.htm
This web site lists several other sites that offer information about multicultural children's literature and other books for grades K–12.

National Clearinghouse for English Language Acquisition (NCELA; formerly NCBE, the National Clearinghouse for Bilingual Education)
www.ncela.gwu.edu
This site offers a wealth of information. The clearinghouse collects, analyzes, synthesizes, and disseminates information about language instruction programs for English language learners and related programs.

National Council of Teachers of English
www.ncte.org
The National Council of Teachers of English site includes numerous resources on teaching literature and children's literature.

National Institute for Urban School Improvement
http://urbanschools.org

This site provides numerous resources, including professional development materials, an online library, position statements, syntheses of research, and other reports.

National Research Center on Learning Disabilities
www.nrcld.org
This site includes lots of information about teaching students with learning disabilities, such as reports from an RTI model research site. There are numerous free downloads, including resource kits.

Reading Rockets
www.readingrockets.org
The Reading Rockets web site includes resources on strategies for working with struggling readers, techniques for teaching reading, and sources for finding recommended books and authors. Helpful podcasts, videos, webcasts, reading-related blogs, and information specific to teachers, families, and other professionals are also available. The site also contains links to information and resources on professional development opportunities (such as "Comprehension: Helping ELLs Grasp the Full Picture").

Read Write Think
www.readwritethink.org
The Read Write Think web site is sponsored by the International Reading Association and the National Council of Teachers of English. It provides a variety of reading information, including lessons, standards, resources, and student materials.

Regional Resource and Federal Center (RRFC) Network
www.rrfcnetwork.org
This web site provides access to an extensive database with information on many other topics ranging from inclusion and early intervening services to parental involvement and Response to Intervention.

Response to Intervention Action Network
www.rtinetwork.org
This site offers information on the effective implementation of Response to Intervention in school districts across the nation. Additional information focuses on specific audiences: pre-K, K–5, middle school, high school, parents, and families.

Response to Intervention Resource Center

www.autoskill.com/intervention/rti.php

This site offers helpful primers on the Response to Intervention (RTI) model, including frequently asked questions. It also includes links to academic research sites, professional associations, resource sites, and published RTI resources. Additional information explains how AutoSkill aligns to RTI.

Rethinking Schools

www.rethinkingschools.org

This web site provides access to in-depth special collections on relevant topics, including one on bilingual education and another on minority student education. It also offers links to numerous publications on various educational issues.

Teaching Tolerance

www.tolerance.org/teach/index.jsp

Teaching Tolerance is a project of the Southern Poverty Law Center. This web site is a wonderful source for antihate and antibias materials, kits, and other resources. For anyone who wants to teach in a more culturally responsive way, this site has lots of great information.

Texas Center for Reading and Language Arts

www.texasreading.org

The web site for the Texas Center for Reading and Language Arts at the University of Texas at Austin provides a wide range of resources and materials to download for teaching reading, including information about teaching English language learners.

U.S. Department of Education

www.ed.gov

The web site for the U.S. Department of Education provides research, statistics, information and resources on education. The Teaching Resources section contains links and publications on teaching reading and teaching English language learners.

U.S. Department of Education's Office of English Language Acquisition, Language Enhancement, and Academic Achievement for Limited English Proficient Students

www.ed.gov/about/offices/list/oela/index.html

This Department of Education web site offers information about current programs and access to reports and resources.

U.S. Department of Education's Office of Special Education and Rehabilitative Services
www.ed.gov/about/offices/list/osers/index.html
This is the U.S. federal government's official web site for information about special education services. Links provide access to reports, resources, publications, and products. The site also offers information on statutes, regulations, legislation, and policies related to teaching students with disabilities.

What Works Clearinghouse
http://ies.ed.gov/ncee/wwc
The What Works Clearinghouse evaluates, summarizes, and posts evidence on the instructional practices and programs that work best in education. Topics include beginning reading, early childhood education, and English language learners.

APPENDIX

SUGGESTED PRINT RESOURCES

August, D., & Shanahan, T. (Eds.) (2007). *Developing reading and writing in second-language learners: Lessons from the report of the National Literacy Panel on language-minority children and youth*. Mahwah, NJ: Lawrence Erlbaum.

Beck, I. L., McKeown, M. G., & Kucan, L. (2002). *Bringing words to life*. New York: Guilford.

Beck., I. L., McKeown, M. G., & Kucan, L. (2008). *Creating robust vocabulary: Frequently asked questions and extended examples*. New York: Guilford.

Francis, D. J., Rivera, M., Lesaux, N., Kieffer, M., & Rivera, H. (2006). *Research-based recommendations for instruction and academic interventions: Practical guidelines for the education of English language learners*. Houston: Center on Instruction.

Freeman, D., & Freeman, Y. (2007). *English language learners: The essential guide*. New York: Scholastic.

Genesee, F., Lindholm-Leary, K., Saunders, W., & Christian, D. (Eds.). *Educating English language learners: A synthesis of research evidence*. Cambridge: Cambridge University Press.

Gentile, L. (2004). *The oracy instructional guide*. Carlsbad, CA: Dominie Press.

Haager, D., Dimino, J., & Windmueller, M. (1997). *Interventions for reading success*. Baltimore: Brookes.

Haager, D., & Klingner, J. K. (2005). *Differentiating instruction in inclusive classrooms: The special educators' guide*. Boston: Allyn & Bacon.

Haager, D., Klingner, J. K., & Vaughn, S. (Eds.) (2007). *Evidence-based practices for response to intervention*. Baltimore: Brookes.

Herrera, S., Perez, D. R., & Escamilla, K. (2009). *Teaching reading to English language learners: Differentiated literacies*. Boston: Allyn & Bacon.

Hoover, J. J. (2009). *Differentiating learning differences from disabilities: Meeting diverse needs through multi-tiered response to intervention*. Boston: Allyn & Bacon.

Hoover, J. J. (2009). *RTI assessment essentials for struggling learners*. Thousand Oaks, CA: Corwin.

Hoover, J., Klingner, J. K., Baca, L., & Patton, J. (2007). *Methods for teaching culturally and linguistically diverse exceptional learners*. Upper Saddle River, NJ: Merrill/Prentice Hall.

Jiménez, T. C., & Graf, V. L. (Eds.) (2008). *Education for all: Critical issues in the education of children and youth with disabilities*. San Francisco: Jossey-Bass.

Klingner, J. K., Hoover, J., & Baca, L. (2008). *Why do English language learners struggle with reading? Distinguishing language acquisition from learning disabilities*. Thousand Oaks, CA: Corwin Press.

Klingner, J. K., Vaughn, S., & Boardman, A. (2007). *Teaching reading comprehension to students with learning difficulties*. New York: Guilford.

Kress, J. (2008). *The ESL/ELL teacher's book of lists*. San Francisco: Jossey-Bass.

Linan-Thompson, L., & Vaughn, S. (2007). *Research-based methods of reading instruction for English language learners: Grades K–4*. Alexandria, VA: ASCD.

Nash, R. (1999). *NTC's dictionary of Spanish cognates thematically organized*. Columbus, OH: McGraw-Hill.

Peregoy, S. F., & Boyle, O. F. (2008). *Reading, writing, & learning in ESL: A resource book for K–12 teachers* (5th ed.). New York: Addison Wesley Longman.

REFERENCES

CHAPTER ONE

Haager, D., Dimino, J. A., & Windmueller, M. P. (2007). *Interventions for reading success*. Baltimore: Brookes.

CHAPTER TWO

Fradd, S., & Boswell, T. D. (1996). Spanish as an economic resource in metropolitan Miami. *The Bilingual Research Journal, 20*(2), 282–337.

Harry, B., & Klingner, J. K. (2006). *Why are so many minority students in special education? Understanding race and disability in schools*. New York: Teachers College Press.

Martin, B., Jr., Archambault, J., & Ehlert, L. (1989). *Chicka, chicka, boom, boom*. New York: Simon & Schuster.

CHAPTER THREE

Kozol, J. (1991). *Savage inequalities: Children in America's schools*. New York: Crown.

Moll, L.C., Armanti, C., Neff, D., & Gonzalez, N. (1992). Funds of knowledge for teaching: Using a qualitative approach to connect homes and classrooms. *Theory into Practice, 31*(2), 132–141.

Nieto, S. (1999). *The light in their eyes: Creating multicultural learning opportunities*. New York: Teachers College Press.

Orosco, M. J. (2007). *Response to intervention with Latino English language learners*. Unpublished doctoral dissertation, University of Colorado at Boulder.

Sayers-Ward, U. (2005). *La foto del salón*. Baltimore, MD: Success for All Foundation.

Valdés, G. (1996). *Con respeto: Bridging the distances between culturally diverse families and schools*. New York: Teachers College Press.

CONCLUSION

Adelman, H., & Taylor, L. (n.d.). *The relationship of Response to Intervention and systems of learning supports*. Los Angeles: UCLA Center for Mental Health in Schools. Available at http://smhp.psych.ucla.edu/dbsimple.aspx?Primary=2311&Number=9904.

Burdette, P. (2007). *Response to Intervention as it relates to early intervening services*. Alexandria, VA: National Association of State Directors of Special Education, Project Forum.

August, D., & Hakuta, K. (1997). *Improving schooling for language-minority children: A research agenda*. Washington, DC: National Academies Press.

August, D., & Shanahan, T. (Eds.) (2007). *Developing reading and writing in second-language learners: Lessons from the report of the National Literacy Panel on language-minority children and youth*. Mahwah, NJ: Lawrence Erlbaum.

Gersten, R., & Baker, S. (2000). What we know about effective instructional practices for English-language learners. *Exceptional Children*, *66*, 454–470.

Gersten, R., & Jiménez, R. (1998). *Promoting learning for culturally and linguistically diverse students: Classroom applications from contemporary research*. Belmont, CA: Wadsworth.

Graves, A., Gersten, R., & Haager, D. (2004). Literacy instruction in multiple-language first-grade classrooms: Linking student outcomes to observed instructional practice. *Learning Disabilities Research and Practice*, *19*, 262–272.

Klingner, J., Méndez Barletta, L., & Hoover, J. (2008). Response to intervention models and English language learners. In J. K. Klingner, J. Hoover, & L. Baca (Eds.), *English language learners who struggle with reading: Language acquisition or learning disabilities?* (pp. 37–56). Thousand Oaks, CA: Corwin Press.

Ladson-Billings, G. (1994). *The dreamkeepers: Successful teachers of African American children*. San Francisco: Jossey-Bass.

Ortiz, A. A. (2001). *English language learners with special needs: Effective instructional strategies*. Washington, DC: ERIC Education Reports.

INDEX

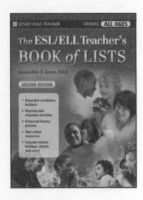

The ESL/ELL Teacher's Book of Lists

2nd Edition

By: **Jacqueline E. Kress, Ed.D.**

ISBN 978-0-470-22267-6
Paperback | 384 pp.

"Includes useful tools, resources, and activities for educators teaching English language learners at any age and across subject area domains. Teachers will find this book helpful in planning lessons and activities that will engage and enrich the language development of ELL students. It will also help teachers to design activities to directly teach the skills English language learners need to be successful."
—Diane Haager, Ph.D., professor, California State University, Los Angeles

This second edition of the bestselling resource includes scores of practical, helpful lists that can be reproduced for classroom students or provide a basis for developing instructional materials and lessons. ESL/ELL teachers K-12 at all instructional levels will find teachable content, key words, and important concepts that help to reinforce and enhance grammar, vocabulary, pronunciation, and writing skills for all ESL students no matter what their ability level or what approach is used.

Completely revised and updated, this new edition includes myriad new lists that reflect the latest information and resources for teaching English language learners in varied subject areas. Designed for easy use and quick access, the lists may be photocopied for individual or group instruction and are organized into the following sections:

- Getting Started
- Culture
- Core English
- Teaching

- Pronunciation
- Content Area Words
- Vocabulary Builders
- Helpful Resources and References

- Grammar
- Glossary
- Assessment

Jacqueline E. Kress, Ed.D., is dean and professor of education at Georgian Court University where she works with college and school faculty to prepare classroom teachers, ESL teachers, reading specialists, special educators, school counselors and administrators. She is coauthor of the bestselling book *The Reading Teacher's Book of Lists* from Jossey-Bass.

The Reading Teacher's Book of Lists

5th Edition

By: **Edward B Fry, Ph.D.** and
Jacqueline E. Kress, Ed.D.

ISBN 978-0-7879-8257-7
Paperback | 544 pp.

"The Reading Teacher's Book of Lists *should be on the bookshelf of every reading teacher in the English-speaking world! It is a tremendous resource that I have used over and over again throughout my career. The fifth edition is the best yet! It has more useful information than any of the previous editions. You can be assured that I will make good use of Dr. Fry and Dr. Kress's classic book."*
—Timothy Rasinski, Ph.D., professor of education, Kent State University

Written for anyone who teaches reading, *The Reading Teacher's Book of Lists* is the thoroughly revised edition of the best-selling foundational reading reference book. This classic resource is filled with 218 up-to-date lists teachers can use to develop instructional materials and plan lessons that might otherwise take years and much effort to acquire. The book is organized into eighteen sections that are brimming with practical examples, key words, teaching ideas, and activities that can be used as is or adapted to meet the students' needs. This revised fifth edition contains a complete overhaul of teaching methods sections and includes new sections on electronic resources, new literacies, building fluency, and reading in content areas. The lists are designed to be photocopied as needed for individual, small group or large group use.

Edward B. Fry, Ph.D., Professor Emeritus of Education at Rutgers University (New Brunswick, NJ) where, for 24 years, he was director of the Reading Center. At Rutgers, Dr. Fry taught graduate and undergraduate courses in reading, curriculum, and other educational subjects, and served as chairman and dissertation committee member for doctoral candidates in reading and educational psychology.

Jacqueline E. Kress, Ed.D., is dean and professor of education at Georgian Court University where she works with college and school faculty to prepare classroom teachers, ESL teachers, reading specialists, special educators, school counselors and administrators. She is coauthor of *The ESL Teacher's Book of Lists* from Jossey-Bass.

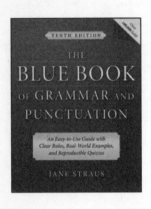

The Blue Book of Grammar and Punctuation

An Easy-to-Use Guide with Clear Rules, Real-World Examples, and Reproducible Quizzes

10ᵗʰ Edition

By: **Jane Straus**

ISBN 978-0-470-22268-3
Paperback | 176 pp.

"Never has there been such a well-arranged, easily navigated guidebook as this.... One of the most practical, useable, beneficial resources, it doubles both as a quick reference guide and student workbook (with answers in the back)!"

—The Old Schoolhouse Magazine

The Blue Book of Grammar and Punctuation is filled with easy-to-understand rules, real-world examples, dozens of reproducible exercises, and pre- and post-tests. This handy workbook is ideal for teachers, students in middle school through college, ESL students, homeschoolers, and professionals. Valuable for anyone who takes tests or writes reports, letters, Web pages, e-mails, or blogs, *The Blue Book* offers instant answers to everyday English usage questions.

Jane Straus has created the popular Web site www.Grammarbook.com, which offers additional self-scoring, downloadable quizzes, video lessons, and a weekly online newsletter full of helpful tips. Jane is also a personal life coach and the author of *Enough Is Enough!* from Jossey-Bass. She keynotes at educational conferences and workshops, writes articles for publication, and appears frequently on TV and radio for her expertise in communications, relationships, and lifestyle enhancement.

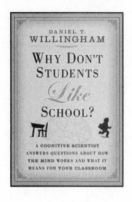

Why Don't Students Like School?

A Cognitive Scientist Answers Questions About How the Mind Works and What It Means for the Classroom

By: **Daniel T. Willingham**

ISBN 978-0-470-27930-4
Hardcover | 192 pp.

"But Mr. Willingham's answers apply just as well outside the classroom. Corporate trainers, marketers and, not least, parents—anyone who cares about how we learn—should find his book valuable reading."

—*Wall Street Journal*

"Just like his Ask the Cognitive Scientist *column, Dan Willingham's book makes fascinating but complicated research from cognitive science accessible to teachers. It is jam packed with ideas that teachers will find both intellectually rich and useful in their classroom work."*

—Randi Weingarten, president, American Federation of Teachers

Kids are naturally curious, but when it comes to school it seems like their minds are turned off. Why is it that they can remember the smallest details from their favorite television program, yet miss the most obvious questions on their history test?

Cognitive scientist Dan Willingham has focused his acclaimed research on the biological and cognitive basis of learning and has a deep understanding of the daily challenges faced by classroom teachers. This book will help teachers improve their practice by explaining how they and their students think and learn—revealing the importance of story, emotion, memory, context, and routine in building knowledge and creating lasting learning experiences.

Daniel T. Willingham is professor of psychology at the University of Virginia, where he has taught since 1992. He writes the popular Ask the Cognitive Scientist column for *American Educator* magazine.

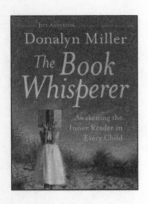

The Book Whisperer

Awakening the Inner Reader in Every Child

By: **Donalyn Miller**

ISBN 978-0-470-37227-2
Paperback | 240 pp.

"Miller is one of those teachers you always wanted for your children. She understands how to teach reading, but knows that is not the same thing as knowing how to LOVE reading. She explores the sources of that love. Few authors have ever conveyed this as well to parents and teachers as Miller does here."

—Jay Mathews, *Washington Post* education columnist and author

Library Journal Starred Review

"Her approach is simple yet provocative. Miller provides many tips for teachers and parents and includes a useful list of ultimate reading suggestions picked by her students. This outstanding contribution to the literature is highly recommended for teachers, parents, and others serving young students."

—Mark Bay, Univ. of the Cumberlands Library, (*Library Journal*, March 15, 2009)

Donalyn Miller says she has yet to meet a child she couldn't turn into a reader. No matter how far behind Miller's students might be when they reach her 6th grade classroom, they end up reading an average of 40 to 50 books a year. Miller's unconventional approach dispenses with drills and worksheets that make reading a chore. Instead, she helps students navigate the world of literature and gives them time to read books they pick out themselves. Her love of books and teaching is both infectious and inspiring. The book includes a dynamite list of recommended "kid lit" that helps parents and teachers find the books that students really like to read.

Donalyn Miller (Bedford, TX) teaches 6th grade language arts and social studies at Trinity Meadows Intermediate School in Keller, Texas. Her popular blog, "The Book Whisperer," is hosted by www.teachermagazine.org